THE AMERICAN SAILING ASSOCIATION'S
COASTAL CRUISING MADE EASY

THE OFFICIAL MANUAL OF THE AMERICAN SAILING ASSOCIATION'S
BASIC COASTAL CRUISING STANDARD (ASA103)

Produced for ASA by

Amanda Lunn Design and Publishing

art editor Sharon Rudd

indexer Penelope Kent

proofreader Paul Massey

First published by American Sailing Association in 2012

American Sailing Association
5301 Beethoven Street, Suite #265
Los Angeles, CA 90066

ISBN 978-0-9821025-1-0

Printed in the U.S.

Learning to sail is just the beginning.

Become a member today and make your sailing lifestyle richer. Let's sail off together on an incredibly fun ASA flotilla, take a bareboating course, or let us help you charter the boat of your dreams from one of ASA's hundreds of affiliates worldwide. Scan here (or visit www.asa.com) for more information on all the great benefits that ASA membership has to offer.

www.asa.com

CONTENTS

THE AMERICAN SAILING ASSOCIATION	4
THE AIM OF THIS BOOK	5
CONTRIBUTORS	6
INTRODUCTION	8
FOREWORD	11

Chapter 1
THE MAGIC OF CRUISING — 12

THE CRUISING SAILBOAT	14
A CRUISING SAILBOAT'S CABIN	18
A SAILBOAT'S EQUIPMENT AND SYSTEMS	22

Chapter 2
MOTORING FUNDAMENTALS — 26

BEFORE GETTING UNDER WAY	28
PRE-DEPARTURE PREPARATIONS	32
MANEUVERING UNDER POWER	34
THE OUTBOARD MOTOR	40
REVIEW QUESTIONS	44

Chapter 3
THE CRUISING LIFE — 46

SAFETY IS PARAMOUNT	48
ON-DECK SAFETY	50
ADDITIONAL SAFETY EQUIPMENT	52
CARE AND FEEDING OF AN AUXILIARY ENGINE	54
LIVING QUARTERS	56
SAILING DYNAMICS	60
WORKING SMART WITH SAILS	62

Chapter 4
KNOW YOUR SAILS AND TRIM 64

LINE-HANDLING EQUIPMENT 66

BEFORE SAILING 68

SETTING SAIL 70

THE FINER POINTS OF SAIL TRIM 72

REEFING UNDER WAY 76

SAILING IN SPECIAL SITUATIONS 78

REVIEW QUESTIONS 80

Chapter 5
RULES AND TOOLS FOR NAVIGATORS 82

THE NAVIGATION RULES 84

SAILING IN REDUCED VISIBILITY 90

AIDS TO NAVIGATION 92

THE NAUTICAL CHART 94

THE SHIP'S COMPASS 96

THE COMPASS AND THE CHART 97

DISTANCE, SPEED, AND TIME 98

ELECTRONIC NAVIGATION 99

Chapter 6
HANDS-ON CRUISING 100

THE COMPASS AT WORK 102

ORIENTATION ON THE WATER 106

ANCHORING 108

ANCHOR WATCH 112

DOCKING MANEUVERS UNDER POWER 114

MOORINGS 122

REVIEW QUESTIONS 124

Chapter 7
SEAMANSHIP 126

MARINE WEATHER 128

ELECTRONIC COMMUNICATIONS 134

HANDLING EMERGENCIES 136

MAN OVERBOARD 142

Chapter 8
ACHIEVING INDEPENDENCE 150

PLANNING A SHORT CRUISE 152

PUTTING THE SAILBOAT TO BED 156

A PARTING KNOT 160

PURSUE THE DREAM 162

REVIEW QUESTIONS 164

APPENDIX 166
GLOSSARY 169
INDEX 174
ANSWERS TO REVIEW QUESTIONS 176

THE AMERICAN SAILING ASSOCIATION

The American Sailing Association was founded in 1983 with a simply stated mission: to teach people to sail safely and confidently. To achieve that goal, the ASA set out to establish standards against which to measure a sailor's level of knowledge and skill, the first such unified standards in the USA to apply to sailors in keelboats.

After studying programs offered in other countries, the founders of the ASA selected the Canadian Yachting Association's (CYA) "Learn to Cruise" program and licensed it for use in the US. With this strong heritage behind it, the ASA has continually improved and expanded its educational system by drawing on valuable input from the ASA school network.

Today, the ASA is an association of sailing schools, charter companies, professional sailing instructors, and sailors, with over 300 affiliated sailing schools located throughout the United States, as well as in Europe, Japan, Central America, Taiwan, China, and other Far Eastern countries. These accredited schools offer ASA certification to individuals who meet the requirements for a given level.

This book, *Coastal Cruising Made Easy,* is the textbook for Basic Coastal Cruising, the second of the eight primary levels of student certification within the ASA system. If you are currently taking sailing classes with an ASA School, you're probably already familiar with *Sailing Made Easy,* the official text for ASA's first-level course, Basic Keelboat. Once you've successfully completed the written and practical on-the-water exams for this second level, you'll be ready to enroll in ASA's Bareboat Chartering course where you will gain the knowledge, confidence, and résumé to skipper boats virtually anywhere in the world.

Whether your goal is to charter a boat in Tahiti or to crew confidently on a short weekend sail, the ASA's sailing-education system will guide you as you learn the theory behind sailing, practice the skills needed to handle a sailboat, and build the foundation of knowledge that will enable you to navigate a vessel safely and within the law.

By establishing national standards for sailing education, the ASA has provided a way for more people to take part in the sport safely, with the proper training and respect for their responsibilities as boaters, ensuring that sailing will be safer, smarter, and more fun for everybody.

For more information please visit our website at www.asa.com.

Charlie Nobles
ASA EXECUTIVE DIRECTOR

THE AIM OF THIS BOOK

The primary purpose of *Coastal Cruising Made Easy* is to serve as the textbook for the American Sailing Association's Basic Coastal Cruising course (ASA103), the second level in ASA's keelboat course progression. ASA103 immediately follows the beginning level, Basic Keelboat (ASA101), and this book builds on the information presented in the textbook for that course, *Sailing Made Easy*.

This book is also appropriate for anyone with a basic working knowledge of sailing who seeks to sharpen his or her skills in order to day sail a bit farther from familiar waters. Those who do successfully complete the Basic Coastal Cruising Standard for which this book was developed have proven their ability to cruise safely in local and regional waters as both skipper and crew on an auxiliary-powered sailboat of about 25 to 35 feet in length, in moderate winds and sea conditions.

When developing the content for this book, ASA drew on the experience gained by its instructors from the countless teaching hours they have accumulated on and off the water. It's no accident, therefore, that the text closely follows the normal sequence in which students are introduced to the boat in which they will take instruction and the skills they will learn. On-the-water exercises demonstrate the theory and bring sailing to life while providing the student with the practice that builds confidence and promotes safety.

Coastal Cruising Made Easy also serves as the foundation of knowledge for subsequent ASA courses and their textbooks. Two-thirds of students who complete the Basic Coastal Cruising Standard continue on to ASA104, Bareboat Chartering, where they build upon their local sailing skills and are instructed in the more advanced topics necessary to serve as the skipper on a multi-day bareboat charter away from familiar waters — the goal of many novice sailors.

While this book is an excellent teaching tool, no text can substitute for the personal insights and individual attention of an instructor. *Coastal Cruising Made Easy* provides valuable reading in advance of the on-the-water portion of the ASA103 course, support material during it, and a permanent reference to take on future sailing adventures. Review questions conclude four of the book's eight chapters to reinforce the information provided throughout the text and prepare the certificate-bound student for the ASA103 test.

Sailing has its own extensive vocabulary of words and expressions. Whenever a new sailing-specific term appears that was not defined in *Sailing Made Easy*, it is printed in italics and explained, often with the help of an illustration. These words and some other common terms are also included in a glossary (see page 169).

CONTRIBUTORS

ASA would like to acknowledge the contributions of the writers and editors who made this book possible.

EDITORS

Peter Isler is one of America's best known sailors both on and off the water. Since being named Collegiate Sailor of the Year while at Yale University, he has been part of five America's Cup campaigns, winning it twice as navigator aboard Dennis Conner's *Stars & Stripes* and covering it three times on television. He is the author of four books, including the best-selling *Sailing for Dummies* and *Peter Isler's Little Blue Book of Sailing Secrets*. Still active as a professional sailor, Peter is also a popular motivational speaker for corporate audiences. As a director of ASA since 1983, he has devoted a great deal of his time to bringing fresh faces into sailing.

Jeremy McGeary left England on an ebb tide in 1970 and rode it through a five-year spell in the Caribbean charter trade before fetching up in the US, where he turned his attention to designing sailboats and writing for sailing magazines. Another turn of the tide put him in the editorial department at *Cruising World* magazine and he is currently Senior Editor at *Good Old Boat* magazine, a position that keeps him in touch with sailors while allowing time for other writing and editing assignments. In addition to his duties as editor, Jeremy developed much of the book's content, both text and illustrations.

Lenny Shabes is the founder of the American Sailing Association and is currently the Chairman of the Board. His first sailing experience was maneuvering a model boat on a lake in Central Park at age 8. Hooked for life, he has since raced and cruised around the world. He has been a boat broker, sailing instructor, and charter-boat captain. He has owned a sailing school and a charter company and has generally been involved in the marine industry for over 35 years. He and his wife, Cindy, currently own a J/100 that they race and day sail out of Marina del Rey, California.

WRITERS

Harry Munns began sailing as a boy in his native Massachusetts. His love of the ocean took him to southern California where he began sailing, teaching, and working as a professional captain. He was one of the founders of the American Sailing Association, and in his 20-year career at ASA, Harry has trained hundreds of instructors around the world. He has written for and contributed to many boating publications and wrote the popular book, *Cruising Fundamentals*. He continues to sail, lecture, and write whenever time allows. Harry was the lead writer for the initial draft of this book.

Bob Diamond began his sailing career in the early 1970s when he was drafted as a sailing instructor at the summer camp where he was a counselor. From that time on, sailing became an obsession. After working as an elementary school teacher in San Jose, California, in 1984, Bob switched to teaching sailing full time at Spinnaker Sailing in Redwood City and has been a sailing instructor ever since. Bob is also a United States Coast Guard (USCG) licensed Master, and an ASA Instructor Evaluator.

Tom Landers has been an avid sailor and charter captain for 40 years while cruising and racing on Chesapeake Bay. He has taught sailing professionally with ASA for over a decade and founded an ASA-certified sailing school in Deltaville, Virginia. Captain Tom has won several awards, as an ASA instructor, as an ASA school owner, and at the University of Richmond where he has taught sailing for many years. Because of his thorough knowledge of sailing, ASA selected him as the sailing-subject-matter expert for several sailing-related consulting projects.

Mary Swift-Swan began sailing in 1980 and a few years later decided that she wanted to teach sailing. She became a certified ASA instructor in 1985 and in the same year became a USCG licensed Captain. She opened her first sailing school in 1987 in Benicia, California, and worked with other schools to develop new programs, including courses for women. In 1997, Mary became the first female ASA Instructor Evaluator. Today, she co-owns Afterguard Sailing Academy in Oakland with her husband, where they are developing an incentive program for high-schoolers.

Lan Yarbrough has been teaching ASA courses professionally since 1989 in places as far apart as Chesapeake Bay and the Nile River. While in Cairo, he was chief instructor for the Cairo Yacht Club and was nominated as a national sailing coach for Egypt. Lan, who had been sailing for a long time, only got truly serious about it when he went to an ASA instructor for professional training and learned something new in every class. He is now a partner in Live and Learn Sailing, a California sailing school, where he indulges his great passion for teaching marine navigation in its traditional and electronic forms.

photography

Billy Black has been called an artist with a camera. He started his career in photography in the New York fashion industry but quickly discovered that he preferred action and traveling to new places and capturing the magic of the light and the spirit of the people. He sailed his Ericson 39 into Newport for the start of the 1986 BOC Challenge and moved to Rhode Island in 1991. Billy works out of his office in Portsmouth, Rhode Island, with his wife, Joyce, and assistant, Meagan Beauchemin. He specializes in publicity work for all kinds of boats but also enjoys destination and adventure-sailing photography.

artwork

Peter Bull has worked as a freelance illustrator for over 25 years. His studio has produced illustrations for sailing manuals for many years. Peter works from his studio (Peter Bull Art Studio) based at his home in Wadhurst, East Sussex, England, with illustrators and designers creating work for the publishing and advertising industries worldwide.

ACKNOWLEDGEMENTS

ASA is also deeply grateful to the following people who have contributed their knowledge, guidance, and time to the realization of *Coastal Cruising Made Easy*:

Charlie Nobles Executive Director
Jeff Riecks Instructor
Cynthia Shabes President
Brenda Wempner Education Coordinator

Dave Lumian Government and Regulatory Liaison
Andy Batchelor Instructor
Lisa Batchelor Frailey Instructor
Reed Freyermuth Founding Board Member

Thanks also to **Hunter Marine** for arranging the loan of the Hunter sailboats used for photography and **Narragansett Sailing** for providing the boats.

INTRODUCTION

Congratulations! You are about to take the next step on the (figurative) road to becoming a proficient sailor. For me, part of the continuing appeal of sailing is the breadth of the challenge that it presents. Not only will we never fully master all of the skills sailing calls for, but our skills and knowledge are tested in new ways every time we go sailing. Sailors share a common bond; the love of being on the water, the thrill of manipulating the wind and challenging our boundaries to see what's around the next point, and the next. Sailing gives us the means to venture outside our safe zone, our harbor, and follow the earliest sailors who explored beyond the horizon — the edge of a supposedly flat world where the charts warned, "Here there be dragons."

Before you can sail to the edge of the world and beyond, you will need to master a broad mix of skills. A sailor must have an understanding of the water, wind, tides, currents and, of course, the weather. This book will help you do that. I hope you enjoy it.

None of this would be possible without the thousands of professional ASA instructors who labor to impart their love of the sea to you. I thank all of you who teach and give a little part of yourselves to enrich the world of sailing.

Lenny Shabes
ASA CHAIRMAN OF THE BOARD

FOREWORD

"To reach a port, we must sail — sail, not tie at anchor — sail, not drift."

Franklin D. Roosevelt

A sailor really never stops learning. That's one of the great things about the sport. You start out in familiar waters on (usually) a small boat and, if you persist, you can build your abilities to the point where you are exploring places that few people on the planet will ever experience in a boat that can safely carry you and the crew across oceans. For some, the wanderlust doesn't tug so hard, but they become interested in honing their skills at navigation, or enjoy a lifetime of sailing in their home waters, often when the wind is blowing so hard others are furling sails and heading in. The bottom line is that sailing offers such a diversity of experiences that you can tack and jibe your sailing career through many many years to come – as long as you keep learning.

If you are progressing from ASA's Basic Keelboat standard to the Basic Coastal Cruising standard, you are ready to up the "degree of difficulty" of your sailing. From the familiar boat in your familiar waters, you are setting your boundaries a bit farther afield. You will learn about operating a bigger boat and its systems and sharpen your sailing skills as you sail in more challenging weather conditions.

The key to learning sailing is to really master the basic skills before you press onward. That's why the ASA system is structured in steps. Take the time to really understand the lessons at each step, then spend as many hours as you can building and refining the skills you just learned before moving on to the next leg of your journey. Do not rush this process — enjoy it. Any old salt will tell you that you have a lifetime of fun and learning ahead of you.

As you move along in building your own sailing skills, you will also inherit more responsibility for the boat and your crew. On a boat — especially in a challenging situation — the crew look to those with more experience for comfort, guidance, and leadership. Remember that the skills you are learning are not just for you — they are important for everyone you sail with — family, friends, and shipmates.

Fair winds and smooth seas,

Peter Isler

Peter Isler
TWO-TIME AMERICA'S CUP-WINNING NAVIGATOR AND
A FOUNDING DIRECTOR OF THE ASA

CHAPTER 1

The magic of cruising

A sailboat is the nearest thing to a magic carpet that we can hope to achieve within the laws of nature. It draws energy from the surrounding air and converts it into a propulsive force. As long as there is wind, and water to float it, a sailboat will take us anywhere we care to go.

Some sailors are content if that anywhere is a lake or estuary near home. But the urge to explore is deep within our genes, and human ingenuity has yet to come up with a vehicle as capable as the sailboat of sustaining a crew of explorers in regions far from sources of fuel and food.

A well-built, well-equipped, and well-stocked sailboat will take a well-prepared crew to the tropics, the Arctic, and anywhere in between. For those who dream of making such an adventure, the voyage begins with laying the foundation of knowledge on which to build it.

THE CRUISING SAILBOAT

What is a cruising sailboat? Simply, it's any sailboat used for traveling from place to place by water. Whether big or small, cruising boats have living quarters and some creature comforts. In this book, we'll get familiar with and learn to sail and operate a boat between 30 and 35 feet in length. That's big enough to provoke dreams of ocean passages but small enough for exploring the bays and rivers where most novice sailors get their first taste of cruising.

A TYPICAL CRUISING BOAT

Sailboats come in many shapes, sizes, and forms to meet the needs of sailors with a variety of desires and ambitions. They also reflect the styles and ideas of their designers and builders and are considered by some sailors to be an art form. The illustrations in this book depict a boat — "our boat" — about 33 feet long of fairly typical design above and below deck and fitted with basic systems commonly found on cruising boats. Throughout the book, photographs of many different boats show how diverse the variations in design and internal and external arrangements can be.

EFFECTS OF SCALE

If you learned to sail on a smaller daysailing keelboat, you'll notice as soon as you step aboard this boat that it's more stable. That's because it's bigger and heavier. Your weight is less relative to the weight of the boat, so the boat is less sensitive to where you stand or sit. By the same token, it takes more effort to move this boat. That means the loads on the sails and rigging are proportionately higher and, in turn, the gear used to set and trim the sails is bigger, stronger, and heavier than that on the daysailing keelboat.

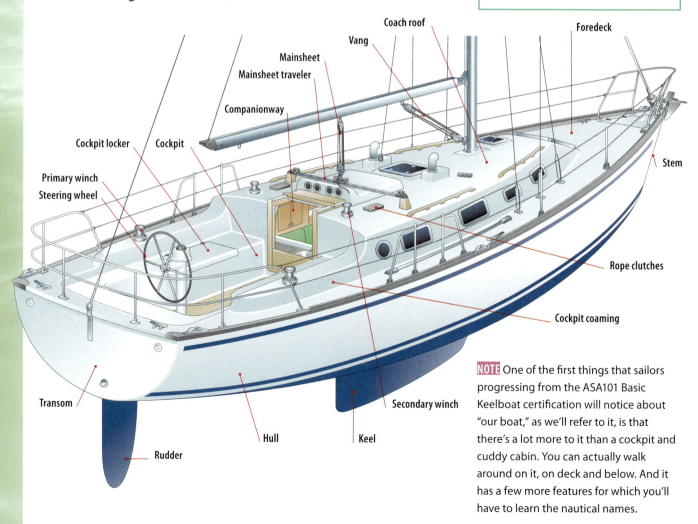

Coach roof
Foredeck
Vang
Mainsheet
Mainsheet traveler
Companionway
Cockpit locker
Cockpit
Stem
Primary winch
Steering wheel
Rope clutches
Cockpit coaming
Transom
Secondary winch
Hull
Keel
Rudder

NOTE One of the first things that sailors progressing from the ASA101 Basic Keelboat certification will notice about "our boat," as we'll refer to it, is that there's a lot more to it than a cockpit and cuddy cabin. You can actually walk around on it, on deck and below. And it has a few more features for which you'll have to learn the nautical names.

THE HELM

Where the smaller daysailers used for ASA Basic Keelboat courses most often have a tiller, this boat has a steering wheel. While it's possible to steer this big a boat with a tiller, and many sailors prefer the feel and response it gives when sailing, the tiller needed to provide sufficient leverage would be quite long. The wheel provides the same or even more leverage while taking up much less space in the cockpit — much of the linkage system that connects it to the rudder is beneath the cockpit.

After stepping aboard a sailboat, who doesn't want to immediately stand behind the steering wheel? With eager crew at their stations, and the commander's view of the boat and its surroundings, it's easy to imagine: "So, this is what it feels like to be the skipper!"

THE COCKPIT

The cockpit is *self-bailing* — it's high enough above the waterline that any water that gets into it can drain overboard by gravity. It drains through *scuppers* (they look like large bathtub drains) in the aft corners of the cockpit well.

Cruising is not all tacking and jibing, and the cockpit also serves as the boat's porch, lounge, and even dining room. The seats are designed to provide support and comfort when sailing and at rest. On our boat, they are spaced just far

Everybody likes the feeling of being in control that the view from behind the wheel inspires.

enough apart that, when the boat heels, you can brace your feet on the leeward one while sitting on the windward one. The seat back is also the cockpit *coaming* that forms a sort of wall around the cockpit to keep out any water that might run along the deck.

COCKPIT LAYOUT

When cruising, sailing is only part of the entertainment and, on this boat, the sail-trimming and other boat-handling equipment is laid out to be easy to operate but also in a way that it doesn't impinge on the cockpit's other uses.

You will notice that the mainsheet and traveler are fitted on the *coach roof* forward of the companionway hatch. This arrangement has several benefits for cruising. The mainsheet can't sweep through the cockpit in a jibe, you don't have to climb over the traveler when moving about in the cockpit, and it's easier to fit a sunshade. However, this arrangement has put the mainsail controls out of reach of the helmsman, which means a crewmember will have to be stationed to take charge of them.

On our boat, as on many boats, a large number of lines (halyards and sail controls) lead to winches at the forward end of the cockpit. This is so all the sail handling is done in one convenient location and without the need to go to the mast or foredeck when under way. The lines are led through and held in clutches (which are described in Chapter 4) and can be tensioned and eased using the winches. It all looks a little busy at first but, once you start using them, the

lines will quickly make sense (especially if they are of different colors and the clutches are labeled).

The jibsheets lead to the *primary* winches port and starboard on the cockpit coamings where they are within reach of the helm, which is a great advantage when sailing shorthanded.

COCKPIT STOWAGES

Even our daysailer carried a fair amount of ancillary gear — docklines, fenders, and safety gear — and a boat equipped for cruising carries a great deal more. All this stuff has to go somewhere so it's not underfoot while the boat's sailing. A lot of it goes in the *cockpit lockers*.

On our boat, a hatch in the port-side cockpit seat opens to reveal a deep locker. Typically, such a locker is large enough to hold lots of gear, including an extra sail or two. Keeping it organized can be a challenge but is necessary, not just so you can find a spare line in a hurry but because often the same locker also provides access to some important fixed equipment. On our boat, that's the engine and the steering gear.

Another locker is located under the starboard seat but this one is only shallow because, on our boat, the space below is used as part of the living quarters.

Two more hatches are located in the helm seat. They provide access to the steering gear and other systems.

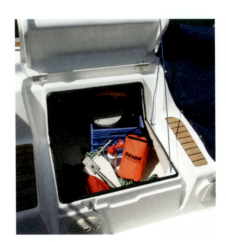
Cockpit lockers are usually the largest storage compartments on the boat — and they fill up fast!

A TOUR OF THE DECK

Even when the boat is tied securely to the dock, the deck presents something of an obstacle course when you try to get around it. Walk, don't run, watch your footing, and take advantage of handholds where they are provided.

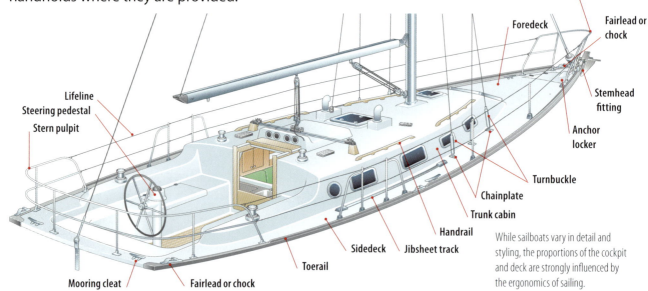

Labels: Bow pulpit · Foredeck · Fairlead or chock · Stemhead fitting · Anchor locker · Turnbuckle · Chainplate · Trunk cabin · Handrail · Jibsheet track · Sidedeck · Toerail · Fairlead or chock · Mooring cleat · Stern pulpit · Steering pedestal · Lifeline

While sailboats vary in detail and styling, the proportions of the cockpit and deck are strongly influenced by the ergonomics of sailing.

SIDEDECK

Your first obstacle when leaving the cockpit to go forward on the deck is the cockpit coaming, which extends aft of the *trunk cabin*, the area of the deck that's raised to provide headroom in the cabin below.

Stepping over the the cockpit coaming brings you onto the *sidedeck*, which runs between the trunk cabin and the outside edge of the deck (which is often referred to as the *rail* because of the *toerail* attached there to provide secure footing).

Just inside the toerail are the stanchions that support the *lifelines*.

Abreast of the mast you will encounter the shrouds, the wires that support the mast laterally. They attach to the deck at the *chainplates* which carry the forces generated by the sails into the structure of the hull.

Between the lower end of each wire shroud and its chainplate is a *turnbuckle*, which is used to tension the shroud by adjusting its length. A *clevis pin* connects the turnbuckle to the chainplate and a *cotter pin* passed through a hole on the end of the clevis pin prevents the clevis pin

from backing out. Cotter pins are also fitted through the screws in the turnbuckles so they cannot unscrew and loosen.

The upper ends of the shrouds are attached to tangs on the mast.

The shrouds terminate at turnbuckles, which are attached to the chainplates with clevis pins.

SAFETY TIP *Remember that, when sailing, the safest path forward is along the windward (high) side of the boat, keeping your weight low at all times. If a task requires you to be on the leeward side, as shown here, take extra care. Use the handrails on top of the cabin for support as they are inboard and more rigid than the lifelines. Remember too, "One hand for the ship and one hand for yourself."*

FOREDECK

When you walk forward of the mast, you come to the *foredeck*. This once was familiar territory for crews involved in changing headsails, but roller-furling sails have all but eliminated the need to go forward while sailing. It's still a nice place to be, though, to bask in the sun, feel the wind, listen to the bow wave, and watch for dolphins.

You'll also use the foredeck when anchoring and docking. Fairleads on each side of the bow direct docklines to two large mooring cleats.

Anchors are heavy and awkward to move around so, on cruising boats that anchor regularly, one anchor is usually stowed on deck in a convenient location from which it can be easily deployed.

On our boat, the anchor stows on the *stemhead fitting*, a hefty stainless-steel fabrication that incorporates a roller fairlead for the anchor rode and the chainplate for the forestay. A hatch in the foredeck covers the anchor locker where the rode is stowed ready for use.

If you stand on the bow in the oft-copied pose from the movie, *Titanic*, you'll understand how the stainless-steel railing around it became known as the *bow pulpit*. As well as giving a sense of security, it serves as a robust anchoring point for the lifelines.

STEERING

Wheel steering has been used on ships for hundreds of years. It was invented because the force needed to steer a large vessel is so great a tiller is impracticable. A wheel can be connected to the rudder via a mechanism that works like a reduction gear to reduce the force the helmsman has to apply to turn the rudder.

A rudder generates large forces so it must be strong, well supported, and easy to turn under load.

Our boat has a spade rudder (see box). Its backbone is its stock, which extends from the top of the rudder and passes up through an opening in the hull. The stock is supported by bearings inside the hull.

If this boat had tiller steering, the tiller would attach to the top of the rudder stock. In fact, the boat does have an *emergency tiller* that fits to the top of the stock so the boat can be steered if the wheel-steering mechanism fails.

Of the many mechanisms employed to connect the wheel to the rudder, the most common uses cables to turn a quadrant (essentially a tiller in the shape of a quarter circle) attached to the rudder stock. The cables are arranged so that turning the wheel to the right causes the boat to turn to starboard, so the effect is the same as in a car. The wheel's axle is held in the *steering pedestal*.

BINNACLE

The steering pedestal provides a convenient place to mount the ship's compass, so it also serves as the *binnacle*. On some boats you might also find the engine controls and navigational instruments mounted on and around the pedestal.

RUDDER TYPES

For centuries, the standard underwater form for sailing vessels, including yachts, was a long keel with the rudder attached to its aft end. While many sailboats exist that have this configuration, most modern yachts have fin keels and their rudders are mounted separately. A *skeg-hung* rudder is supported by a skeg that's integral with the hull. A *spade* rudder is "free standing," supported by its stock inside the hull. The spade rudder has become increasingly common on modern boats.

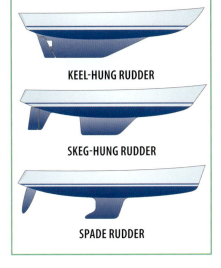

KEEL-HUNG RUDDER

SKEG-HUNG RUDDER

SPADE RUDDER

The stemhead fitting is the chainplate for the forestay. It also supports the anchor storage bracket and the roller fairlead for the anchor rode.

This circular "tiller" (called a radial drive) is bolted to the rudder stock. It's turned by cables that pass under the cockpit and are connected to the steering wheel.

A CRUISING SAILBOAT'S CABIN

Generations of sailors felt that the amenities for living aboard a sailboat need be no better than those expected when camping, save for having the advantages of a deck overhead instead of a leaky tent and a settee to sit or lie on instead of a rock. Times have changed, and modern sailboats, even quite small ones, have many of the comforts of home, albeit scaled down somewhat to fit the shape and proportions of a hull.

THE ACCOMMODATIONS

For many sailors progressing from the ASA Basic Keelboat class, the living quarters on the cruising boat will be a novelty. One of the first priorities, therefore, will be to get a feel for how all the features are arranged and learn their nautical names.

COMPACT AND COMFORTABLE

Our boat's entrance, the *companionway*, is at the forward end of the cockpit. It has a sliding hatch and a short ladder that leads below to the main cabin.

Different areas of the main cabin are dedicated to specific purposes, but because the boat's size and the shape of the hull put a premium on space, many parts fulfill two or even more roles.

One part of the cabin is the *saloon*, where settees are arranged around a central table. This area serves as the living room, the dining room, and the den, and the seating provides additional sleeping quarters for extra crew or guests. Long-distance cruisers might also use the saloon as a workshop or sail-repair loft.

Cruising is a social pastime, and the *galley* (do not use the word kitchen) is open to the saloon so the cook can join the conversation.

In another corner of the main cabin, the *chart table* is dedicated to the needs of the navigator. In the spirit of multipurposing, the navigator's seat might be the head of the *quarter berth*.

Cabins used for sleeping are called staterooms (the term comes from more stately vessels) and beds are berths. The forward stateroom has a *V-berth*, so called because it follows the shape of the hull as it narrows toward the bow.

On a boat, the bathroom is called the head, and on our boat it contains a marine toilet, a hand basin, and a handheld shower, all in the space of your guest-room shower stall at home.

Sailboat interiors are ergonomically designed around a variety of crew activities that take place at rest and under way. They must also accommodate a number of structural requirements.

DIVISIONS AND STOWAGES

Walls that divide the interior of a boat into compartments are called *bulkheads*. Some bulkheads are structural and, on many boats, the main bulkhead that braces the hull against stresses imposed by the mast and rigging is at the forward end of the saloon. Other bulkheads enclose the spaces for the staterooms and head.

The cushions for the berths and saloon settees rest on large flat surfaces and, since no space can be wasted, that beneath them is used for storage. Some of these spaces are divided into bins that can be used for stowing anything and everything you bring aboard the boat: food, spare parts for the engine, safety equipment, even beer (but in cans rather than bottles, please). Others are taken up with tanks — you might find a freshwater tank under the starboard settee or the V-berth, for instance, and a fuel tank under a quarter berth — and other essential components of the boat's domestic systems.

CHART TABLE

Traditionally, the chart table (or navigation table) is the center of operations for the boat both under way and in port. The books, charts, and instruments used in navigation are kept here and, when sailing, the skipper and navigator use it to keep track of the boat's progress and as the communications station. Because it's a desk, in port it naturally becomes the ship's office and its storage compartments are handy repositories for things you want to stay dry, like your cell phone. If you're looking for the engine keys, a notepad, or a flashlight, you'll probably find them in or near the chart table.

On some boats, you might also find bins under hatches in the cabin *sole*. On a boat, you walk on the sole (a floor is a structural member that runs across the boat above the keel, tying together the two sides of the hull). The space in the bottom of the boat beneath the sole is the bilge.

Other storage spaces abound in every available corner of the boat. Lockers are fitted behind settees, around the galley, in the staterooms, and in the head. You'll also find drawers here and there.

Sailing isn't always a dry activity, so some boats have a dedicated *wet locker* where foul weather gear (that kept you dry on deck) can be hung up so it doesn't spread its dampness to the boat's interior.

TIP *What you would call a cabinet at home is a "locker" aboard a boat, because, for its contents to stay in place when the boat is sailing, the door needs a means of keeping it securely closed when the boat heels.*

Smaller boats can be comfortable even when they have just the bare essentials. All but the very smallest have more amenities than a tent.

A modern open-plan arrangement brings all the main functions of a sailboat's saloon, galley, and chart table into one inviting space.

The V-berth is named for its shape, formed by the shape of the boat at the bow.

On a larger boat, the V-berth cabin can be quite spacious and luxurious.

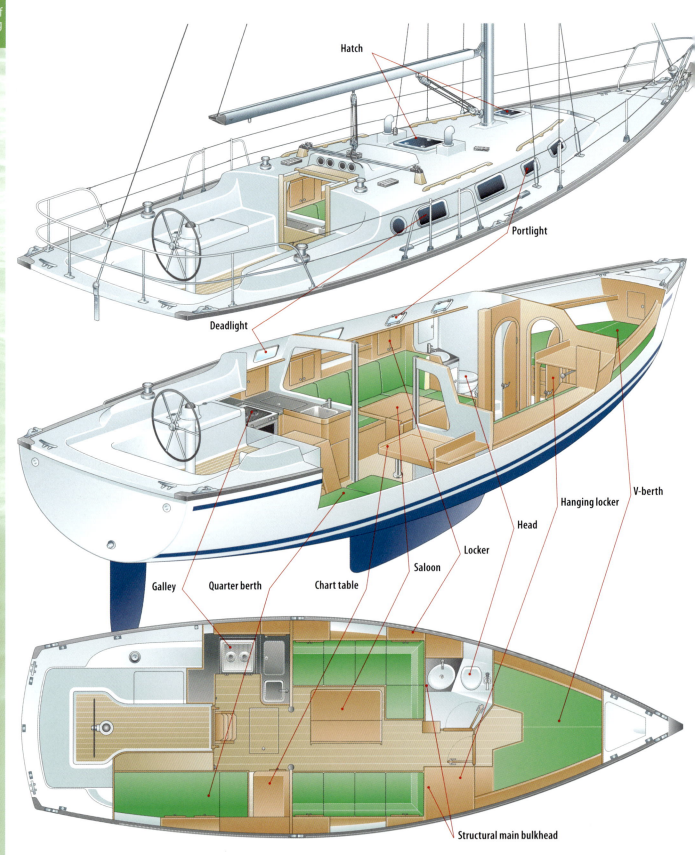

Hatch

Portlight

Deadlight

V-berth

Hanging locker

Head

Locker

Saloon

Chart table

Galley   Quarter berth

Structural main bulkhead

A sailboat encloses the amenities of a weekend cottage inside a structure engineered to withstand the forces imposed by the sea and the sails. Every component is connected in some way with every other. On our boat, for example, if the cockpit were longer, that would impinge on the galley and saloon and might mean relocating the mainsheet traveler.

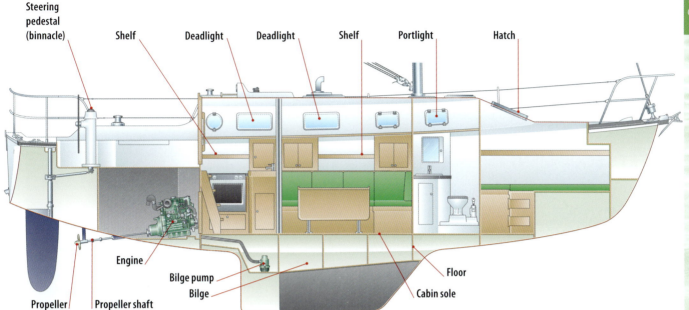

Steering pedestal (binnacle) · Shelf · Deadlight · Deadlight · Shelf · Portlight · Hatch

Engine · Bilge pump · Bilge · Floor · Cabin sole · Propeller · Propeller shaft

LIGHT AND AIR

Light and ventilation are important to comfort aboard, so the more ways you can let both in without also letting in water the better.

Openings cut in the deck are called *hatches* and are often used for access as well as ventilation. Fixed "windows" in the hull or cabin sides are called *deadlights*; ones that open are called *portlights* or *opening ports*. Any such opening is a potential source of a leak, but, happily, all of these fittings today are well-engineered, strong, and generally waterproof (as long as you remember to close them before you go sailing). Our boat has several of each type.

In the cabin sides, it has a mix of portlights and deadlights. Overhead, in addition to the companionway hatch, it has a large opening hatch over the saloon and a smaller one over the head.

As well as admitting light and air to the cabin, portlights add their distinctive nautical character.

Another opening hatch over the V-berth is large enough to be used as a back door or an escape hatch (and it's also big enough to pass a sail through). All the hatches on our boat have tough transparent-plastic lenses to let in light.

DORADE VENTS

No matter how many hatches and lights you have, when they are all closed, as they must be at sea, the cabin can become very close and humid. Olin Stephens came up with a solution when he designed the yacht *Dorade* in 1929. It consists of an air scoop mounted on a box that has baffles inside that allow air to pass but stop rain or airborne spray.

A TYPICAL LAYOUT

As the photos in this book show, boats vary considerably in how they are laid out belowdecks. Our boat, shown here, has a simple layout similar to those found in many cruising boats of this size.

The galley is to port, next to the companionway. Braced inside its U-shaped counters, the cook can reach everything — lockers, bins, sink, and stove.

Opposite the galley is the chart table and, aft of it, the quarter berth. On some designs, a larger berth occupies the width of the boat under the cockpit.

In the saloon, an L-shaped settee surrounds the dining table on the port side. A folding leaf on the table opens to reach the settee on the starboard side when needed. Both settees are long enough to be used as sleeping berths.

Lockers and other storage areas are fitted outboard of and under the settees.

Forward of the saloon, the structural main bulkhead stiffens the boat and divides the accommodations.

Forward of this bulkhead, the head — with toilet, sink, and shower — is on the port side and a hanging locker is fitted on the starboard side.

The V-berth fills the forward stateroom. On a bigger boat, this cabin would have more floor space and storage lockers.

Our boat has an engine. It's located behind the companionway steps.

A SAILBOAT'S EQUIPMENT AND SYSTEMS

By now, you'll be getting the picture that a cruising sailboat can be quite comfortable. It also carries supplies of water, fuel, and food, and has mechanical, plumbing, and electrical systems that enable it to sustain its crew "off the grid" for lengthy periods of time. Once you have your bearings belowdecks, your instructor will show you where some of the boat's essential equipment is located. We'll present an overview here — and see how it all works in due course.

SAFETY EQUIPMENT

You will recall from your basic keelboat experience that federal regulations require boats to carry certain items of equipment for the purpose of protecting lives. Specifications, which vary according to boat size, and related regulations are presented in the Appendix 1 (page 166), which is laid out in the form of a safety-equipment checklist. For now, let's just see where the various items might be kept.

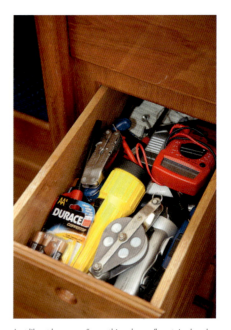

Just like at home, an "everything drawer" contains handy odds and ends. This one is in the chart table.

FIRE EXTINGUISHERS

At 33 feet long, our boat is required to carry one B-II or two B-I extinguishers. The letter B indicates that the extinguisher is rated for petroleum-based fires and that rating is needed because the boat is fiberglass and carries petroleum fuel (diesel for the engine). The federal requirement is a minimum, and since more (and bigger) is better when it comes to safety, and the ASA recommends having a couple of the larger size B-IIs strategically placed in the accommodations and another in a cockpit locker.

EMERGENCY SIGNALS

Because of its length and its ability to operate at night, our 33-foot boat is required to carry signals rated for use in daylight and after dark. Three handheld red flares satisfy both needs but again, "more is better," so it doesn't hurt to add three (or more!) orange smoke daytime signals because, on bright days, they can be more effective than flares.

On our boat, a good place to store these would be in a locker near the chart table, which is handy to the companionway and therefore the cockpit. Other items that can be used for signaling, such as an emergency flag, an air horn (with spare canisters), and flashlights might be kept in the same location.

TIP Remember, every boat is different and exactly where gear is stowed depends on the boat's layout and the skipper's preference. The description here is provided as an example of where items can be stowed.

LIFE JACKETS

Regulations require every boat to carry a Coast Guard-approved life jacket for each person on board, Although the normal complement aboard our boat would be six, prudence requires we carry a few extras in case of company.

Fire extinguishers might not add much to the decor, but being visible is crucial to their utility if needed.

Life jackets might be stowed below while the boat is docked and brought into a cockpit locker for sailing.

PLUMBING AND PUMPS

High on the list of amenities that make our cruising boat livable is its supply of fresh water. To use that water, we need a means to draw it from the tank and ways to dispose of it once we've used it. There's also the matter of unwanted water that gets into the bilge.

FRESH WATER

As soon as you untie your sailboat from the dock you depend on it for everything. One necessity you have to take along with you is fresh water.

Water is heavy and it takes up space, factors that limit how much water a boat can carry. How long that water lasts depends on how carefully you use it. If your cruise takes you to a marina berth each night, you can replenish your supply. When you venture away from civilization, though, you will have to monitor consumption so you don't run out of water.

Most cruising boats have a plumbed water system. Our boat has faucets in the galley and faucets and a shower in the head. These are served by an electric pump with an accumulator and pressure switch (not unlike the arrangement found in a rural home with a well). The pump draws water from the water tank, which, on our boat, is located under the starboard saloon settee with the pump and accumulator adjacent to its aft end. (There's also a hand pump at the galley sink.)

WASTE WATER

The galley sink drains overboard through a *through-hull fitting* in the bottom of the boat. To stop seawater from flooding into the boat in the event the drain plumbing fails, a *seacock*, a valve designed for marine use, is fitted to the through-hull fitting.

The sink in the head drains overboard in a similar way. Note that, on our boat, this sink is well outboard to port and might be below sea level when the boat heels to port. Its seacock should be closed whenever the boat is under way. It's good practice also to close these seacocks if the boat is to be left unattended for an extended period.

To keep soapy water out of the bilge when you shower, the water collects in a sump below the sole and is discharged overboard by an electric pump.

BILGE SYSTEM

Any water that gets into the boat, whether it's seawater or rain through a hatch left open, or fresh water leaking from the boat's own supply, will accumulate in the bilge. To remove it, the boat has a *bilge pump*.

For the sake of redundancy, most boats have at least two bilge pumps. One of them is often an electric pump that's fitted in the deepest part of the bilge (on our boat that's under the sole between the chart table and the galley) and connected to a switch that will turn it on automatically when water rises above a certain level (like a basement sump pump). A hose leads from the same deep area of the bilge to a manual pump fitted in the cockpit. The intakes for both pumps are fitted with strainers to keep out solid matter.

It's normal practice to lift a floorboard from time to time to inspect the bilge, test the pumps, and ensure no debris is clogging the pump intakes.

When a boat's through-hull fittings are located together, it makes it easy to find them when you want to operate the seacocks or check for leaks.

A sump in the bilge houses an automatic bilge pump and a suction for a manual pump. The screen fence around it keeps debris out of the pumps.

ELECTRICAL SYSTEM

Many of the creature comforts that elevate cruising above camping are made possible because a boat can have electricity aboard. In fact, our boat has two separate electrical systems. One of them operates all the time and the other can only be used when the boat is at a dock and connected to a shoreside supply.

The ship's batteries power the lights, pumps, and navigation instruments, and also start the engine.

DC POWER

Electrical equipment on most boats of this size runs off a 12-volt direct current (12VDC) system supplied by batteries.

Our boat has two 12-volt batteries (rather larger than car batteries) located next to the quarter berth. One is the *house* battery, and is used to operate the "house," or boat, services: lights, pumps, and other devices such as navigational instruments. The second battery is for starting the engine. Normally, you run the boat off the house battery to conserve the starting battery's power so you can always start the engine when you need it. When you need to connect the batteries, you do so with the *battery selector switch*.

You can monitor the battery voltage and control electricity usage from the *distribution panel*, or switchboard, which on our boat is located at the boat's nerve center, the chart table. The panel has a switch for each circuit in the boat so that only the circuits in use at any time need be activated. For example, when the lighting circuit is activated with its switch on the distribution panel, individual cabin lights can be turned on and off with their own switches.

Batteries store a finite amount of electrical energy, so you must take care to conserve it (by not leaving on lights or equipment you're not using) unless the engine is running (see facing page) or the boat is "plugged in" to *shorepower*.

....

TIP *Cruising sailors must always be mindful of the state of charge of their batteries.*

....

SHOREPOWER

Many sailboats today have a second electrical system that runs on the same 120-volt alternating current (120VAC) supply as your house. This system has its own distribution panel and only operates when the boat is connected to a *shorepower* outlet on a dock.

A boat with 120VAC will usually have outlets that look similar to those in your home, and you can plug in and use the same appliances — yes, a hair dryer! It will also have a battery charger for maintaining the ship's batteries.

A boat that's connected to shorepower can even be air conditioned, which lets sailors in hot climates stay on their boats in comfort when the day's sailing is over.

Switches on the the electrical panel control separate circuits for the DC and shorepower services.

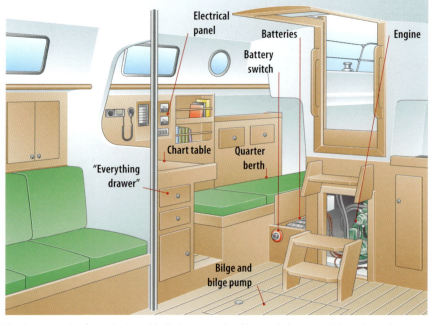

The electrical panel is often at the chart table. The battery switch will be near the batteries, which are close to the engine to keep as short as possible the heavy cables that carry current to the starter.

AUXILIARY PROPULSION

Many sailors have made long voyages without having engines in their boats. Some of them are purists who believe engines don't encourage good seamanship; some simply don't want the noise and the smell in their homes; some had an engine until it died and they haven't got around to fixing it. With very few exceptions, cruising boats today are fitted with auxiliary engines.

The battery selector switch plays a very important role in the boat's electrical system.

THE ENGINE

On our 33-foot boat, the engine is tucked into a rather tight compartment under the cockpit. You can see most of it and reach some of its service points by lifting out the companionway ladder and opening the hatch behind it. To get at the aft end of the engine, where you'll find the transmission and the connection to the propeller shaft, you have to climb into the port cockpit locker.

We'll get into the details of how to start and stop the engine and how to perform some simple service tasks later. For now, it's enough to know where it is and to understand that it has a whole suite of support systems. It has a fuel system, an exhaust system, a cooling system, and an air supply. It also has an alternator.

BATTERY CHARGING

Just like a car, our cruising sailboat has an alternator driven by the engine to produce the electricity needed to charge the batteries that power the 12VDC system. When the boat is away from a dock, the alternator is the only means of charging the batteries. Although it's appealing to always be a sailboat and run the engine only when there's no wind, or for the few minutes it takes to leave the dock, it's sometimes necessary to run it for an hour or so to bring the batteries up to full charge so you can continue to use the lights and other electrical devices on board. To avoid surprises, keep an eye on the voltmeter on the electrical panel that shows the batteries' level of charge—and use the battery selector switch.

BATTERY SELECTOR SWITCH

A simple battery selector switch has four positions: Battery 1, Battery 2, Both, and Off. When the engine is running, it should be on Both so the alternator will charge both batteries. When the engine is not running, switch to 1 or 2 (whichever is your house battery) to preserve a full charge in the starting battery. Never turn the switch to Off while the engine is running as that could cause damage to electrical devices, including the alternator.

Sailboat auxiliary engines tend to be in rather compact quarters and servicing them is sometimes a challenge.

WIND AND SOLAR

When it comes to alternative energy, cruising sailors are old hands and have for decades used wind generators and solar panels to provide electricity. These devices allow them to make long voyages or lie at anchor for extended periods without having to run their engines or enter a marina to charge their batteries.

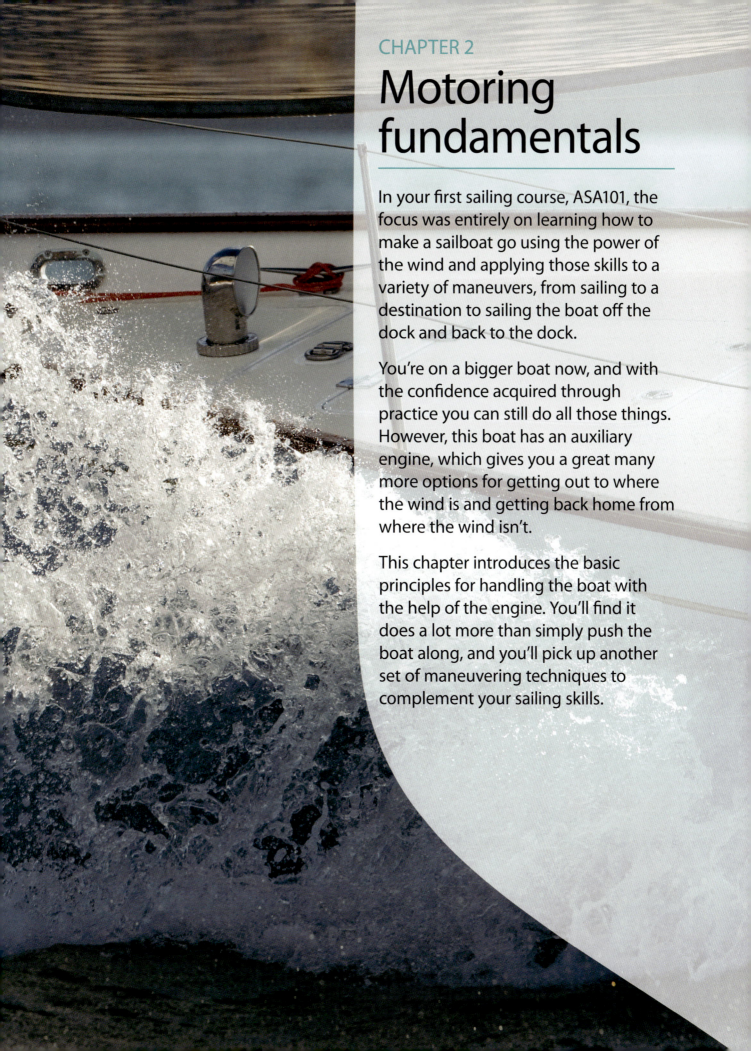

CHAPTER 2

Motoring fundamentals

In your first sailing course, ASA101, the focus was entirely on learning how to make a sailboat go using the power of the wind and applying those skills to a variety of maneuvers, from sailing to a destination to sailing the boat off the dock and back to the dock.

You're on a bigger boat now, and with the confidence acquired through practice you can still do all those things. However, this boat has an auxiliary engine, which gives you a great many more options for getting out to where the wind is and getting back home from where the wind isn't.

This chapter introduces the basic principles for handling the boat with the help of the engine. You'll find it does a lot more than simply push the boat along, and you'll pick up another set of maneuvering techniques to complement your sailing skills.

BEFORE GETTING UNDER WAY

To see just how much auxiliary power adds to your sailboat experience you'll have to take the boat to a suitable area where you can practice maneuvers. But before getting under way for the first time on any boat you want to make sure it's ready for sea and that you are familiar with its systems and how it's set up. After your introductory tour on deck and down below, your instructor will show you how to inspect the boat's equipment and fittings so you can enjoy your time on the water confident the boat is in good shape.

SAFETY INSPECTION

A good place to begin the inspection is with the safety equipment, because the time to discover a fault or deficit is now, while the boat is secure in the dock, and not during an emergency on the water when the equipment is urgently needed.

A horseshoe buoy held in a bracket in the aft pulpit is always ready to be thrown to a MOB at short notice.

BELOWDECKS

On the welcome tour, you saw where the life jackets are stowed. Take them out, count them, and inspect them for signs of wear or damage. Bring any suspected fault to the attention of your instructor, then re-stow the life jackets tidily.

TIP Try on a life jacket and see how it fits. If it makes you feel more comfortable, wear it when the boat gets under way. The ASA recommends the use of PFDs.

Inspect the fire extinguishers to ensure they are secure in their brackets and their gauges show they are properly charged. Read the instructions for their use — you can never do that too many times.

Take the flares out of their container and check their expiration dates, make sure there's a spare canister for the air horn, and test the flashlights. If the boat has a handheld VHF radio, see that its battery is fully charged.

TIP When you become a skipper, on your own or any other boat, you take on responsibility for the safety of your vessel and everyone on board, so these inspections should become routine. If you know your safety equipment is in good condition, you won't need to inspect it before every day sail, but you should show all new crewmembers where it's stowed and how to use it. You could also offer every member of the crew a life jacket to wear should they choose to do so.

MAN-OVERBOARD GEAR

Attached to the lifelines near the stern is a horseshoe buoy or some other device that satisfies the federal requirement that the boat carry a throwable flotation device. This is the first relief for anyone who goes overboard — with luck, whoever sees him go in will be able to throw it to within swimming distance — so the skipper will want to make sure everyone aboard knows where it is and how to release it from its bracket.

In addition to the horseshoe buoy, many boats carry one or more devices specially made to provide flotation to the MOB, make him more visible in the water (a light or a pole with a flag), and even make retrieving him easier (a rescue collar).

Your instructor will point out the equipment on the teaching boat and explain how it works and how it is to be deployed.

TIP A boat sailing at 6 knots leaves behind a MOB at the rate of 10 feet per second. He'll be a boat length astern in the time it takes to grasp the situation, so speed in deploying MOB rescue gear is crucial.

FLARES

AIR HORN

RADIO

LIFE JACKET

FLASHLIGHT

FIRE EXTINGUISHER

One of the first things to do when getting oriented aboard a boat is to become familiar with the safety equipment and where it's stowed.

GENERAL READINESS FOR SEA

When cruising on a sailboat, you take some of the comforts of home along while you enjoy the fun and excitement of sailing and the adventure of visiting new destinations. Sometimes, the sailing part of cruising impacts on the living-aboard part, and vice versa. When it's time to go sailing, the boat must be prepared so that nothing goes amiss when it starts to rock and roll or heel.

STOWING LOOSE ITEMS

You will notice that many horizontal surfaces in the boat's interior and shelves, both inside and outside of lockers, have substantial raised lips around their edges. These are *fiddle rails* and are there to prevent items from sliding off or out when the boat heels to a breeze or rolls in waves. In strategic places, such as around the galley countertops, they are robust enough to be used as handholds.

Gather up all loose items — tableware, books, iPods, etc. — that are lying around on the table or any surface from which they might be launched as projectiles once the boat starts to heel under sail. Stow them securely in lockers or on shelves behind deep fiddle rails.

LOCKERS AND BINS

Make sure that the contents of lockers are secure and that all locker doors are latched. Pay special attention to galley lockers — they are in frequent use and

While the crew on deck have fun sailing, solid fiddle rails and handholds help those moving around belowdecks.

often contain heavy and hard items.

Bins, because their openings are in their tops, are the preferred locations for bulky or heavy items, but stuff can

get lost if they are over filled. If you stow like items together, you'll have an easier time finding them. Bear in mind that the contents of bins low in the boat might get wet if water gets into the bilge.

··

TIP *Stowing stuff in lockers is an art, especially in the galley. You want the contents packed so they can't slide or roll around — the sound can be irritating when the boat's in motion — but also so you can identify everything from just looking in — you don't want to be shuffling things around when the locker is on the high side of a heeled boat.*

··

WATERTIGHT INTEGRITY

Check that all opening ports and deck hatches are firmly closed with the *dogs*, latches, or other devices provided. Seawater is great for sailing on and swimming in but it is not welcome in the living quarters even in the smallest quantities. An open hatch can admit an awful lot of water even on a calm day if you catch a power-boat wake awkwardly.

Check the bilges for water and, if necessary, operate the bilge pump to remove any that has accumulated. Make a note of how much water was there and how long it took to pump out and check back later to see if more water comes in.

Deep lockers hold their contents securely even when the boat's motion is lively, and orderly stowing makes everything visible and accessible.

A securely closed hatch won't let in water. Before getting under way, make sure all hatches and portlights are closed. You're going to be on deck in the fresh air anyway!

ON-DECK INSPECTIONS

Nature wages a continuous campaign of attrition against everything we create, and boats seem to get her special attention. In the pursuit of good seamanship, any prudent sailor will be constantly alert to the condition of his vessel and its equipment. After a while, it becomes instinctive, while going about everyday tasks, to glance around at the boat's hardest-working hardware and equipment, looking for worn stitches on the sail, wear on the jibsheets, or loose bolts on a mast fitting. Even so, it's worth getting into a routine of making a formal tour of inspection.

RIGGING CONNECTIONS

In Chapter 1, we took a quick walk around the deck, but now is a good time to go back and inspect potential trouble spots.

The standing rigging is subject to heavy loads, so that's a good place to start. Whenever the boat tacks, the jib or its sheets drag across the shrouds near the turnbuckles. This can lead to problems — for the sail if the sharp ends of cotter pins are exposed and for the rig if a pin comes out. Check that the protective tape over the cotter pins is intact and that no pins are missing or damaged. Examine the headstay and backstay too.

Make the same examination at the ends of the lifelines where they connect to the pulpits at the bow and the stern. Here, a missing cotter pin, frayed lashing, or loose turnbuckle could lead to someone falling overboard if the lifeline comes undone.

Everywhere you see a block (a pulley used in a sail-control system), whether it's at the base of the mast for a halyard or on the boom as part of the mainsheet, ensure it's attached securely. It might have a pin with a cotter ring or a shackle. If the latter, test the shackle pin for tightness — a loose shackle pin always obeys Murphy's Law.

BILGE PUMP

In the cockpit and often within reach of the helm position is the manual bilge pump. We hope never to have to use it in an emergency but, as with any mechanical equipment, it should be tested every now and then to ensure it

SHACKLE SECURITY

Never put all your trust in shackles (and especially stainless-steel ones) because their screw pins have a knack for working loose. Hand tight is not tight enough, so they should always be tightened with a tool, either pliers or a shackle key. For extra security, shackles that do not need to be undone regularly can be seized by winding seizing wire around the shackle body and through the hole in the shackle pin. A seizing on the shackle that connects the anchor to its chain is vitally important to the boat's security when at anchor.

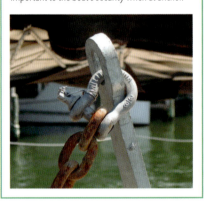

will do its job when needed. Its handle might be tied by a lanyard or stowed in a special bracket mounted inside a cockpit locker so it can't easily be misplaced.

A hose runs from the bilge (remember the strainer under the floorboard?) to the pump's intake. The discharge hose leads to a through-hull above the boat's waterline, often in the transom.

Each of these blocks is attached with a shackle. More shackles are used in the mainsheet and other systems. Every shackle should be checked for tightness on a regular basis.

Almost every sailboat today has a manual bilge pump, similar to this one, mounted in the cockpit. The rules for ocean racing get credit for this safety feature.

Motoring
fundamentals

AT THE CONTROLS

Our boat is fitted with wheel steering, so get behind the wheel to check out the view and the feel. You'll find that the wheel is somewhat of a barrier between you and the rest of the cockpit, where most of the sailing action will take place. You'll see why your instructor, who will take the wheel when you make your first departure from the dock, will be relying on responses and feedback from the crew as you get under way.

STEERING

Steering with a wheel will be a new experience for sailors accustomed to tiller steering. You use the wheel the same way as in a car. When the boat is moving forward and you turn the wheel to the right, the boat's **bow** turns to starboard. When the boat is moving backward (which it can do when motoring) the boat's **stern** turns to starboard.

The cockpit is laid out so you can stand or sit behind the wheel or to one side or the other of it. If your preference when sailing is to steer from the windward side, you can easily duck to leeward to peer behind the jib.

SAILING INSTRUMENTS

Many sailors who start out on a dinghy or a small keelboat learn to gauge the wind's strength and direction and the speed of the boat from sensory feedback provided by the forces felt on the sheets and tiller. Bigger keelboats are heavier and, especially in light or moderate winds, are usually not as responsive as smaller boats. On most boats of this size, the crew get a little assistance from instruments that show the boat's speed through the water and the wind speed and direction. The gauges might be fitted forward of the companionway hatch, where everyone in the cockpit can see them, or on the steering pedestal.

RUDDER AMIDSHIPS

When steering with a tiller, you have an instant reference for the angle the rudder is making with the boat's centerline: Just by looking at it you know how far the rudder is turned. That's important information for the helmsman and the sail trimmer. If the helmsman has to apply "too much helm" to keep the boat sailing on course, that's slow because of the resistance created by the rudder. By adjusting the sails you can reduce helm (or increase it).

Knowing the rudder angle is also important when using the engine to maneuver the boat.

A steering wheel says nothing about the position of the rudder. And, until you get to know a specific boat, when you turn the wheel, you have no idea by how much it's turning the rudder. Here's a way to figure it out while still at the dock.
1. Turn the wheel all the way in one direction until it stops.
2. With the wheel hard over, take hold of it at the top (12 o'clock) and, without taking your hand off, slowly turn it the other way until it stops again, counting the spokes as you go.
3. Turn the wheel all the way back the other way, again counting the spokes.
4. Without removing your hand, turn the wheel back through half the number of spokes you counted.
5. Hold the wheel in that position and mark the 12 o'clock position on the rim with tape.
You can now see when the rudder is amidships and, when it's not, how much "helm" you are giving the boat.

If the rudder stops are not evenly set on both sides, your "top dead center" may be a little biased one way, but it's close enough for a start. You can fine tune it later when under way.

This cockpit is designed with the comfort of the crew in mind as well as to facilitate the sailing. High seatbacks provide support and the jibsheet winch on the coaming is within reach of the helm.

PRE-DEPARTURE PREPARATIONS

Because the engine is new for those who are coming to this boat from a daysailing keelboat, before introducing more advanced sailing topics we'll focus on the engine — how to start it, how to stop it, and how to use forward and reverse gears to maneuver the boat. That doesn't mean we'll ignore the sails; this is a sailboat after all and you have the sails as backup if that lump of machinery should ever decide not to cooperate.

READY THE SAILS

Before starting the engine, prep the boat as if you were going sailing, just as you did on the daysailer: Remove the cover from the mainsail and stow it. Attach the halyard and tie it down with a sail tie. Uncoil the mainsheet, traveler control lines, jibsheets, and the jib's furling line.

THE ENGINE'S CONTROLS

NOTE Because the vast majority of inboard engines in sailboats are diesels, we'll limit the discussion here to starting and stopping a diesel engine. The procedure for a gasoline engine is in the Appendix.

The location and design of engine controls varies from boat to boat. On our boat, the engine controls and instrument panel are on the face of the cockpit seat, just to starboard of the wheel. The panel has a tachometer, an ammeter, a couple

of indicator lights, a key switch, a start button, and a stop control.

Near the panel is a lever that operates the throttle and the gear shift. On other boats you might find the throttle and gear shift (which may be separate or combined on one lever) mounted on the steering pedestal. Your instructor will show you exactly how to operate the particular controls on the boat you are learning on.

An engine requires maintenance, and we'll cover the basics along with the boat's other systems in Chapter 3. For now, we'll assume that the engine's fluids and fuel supply are all in order.

A very important step to take before starting the engine is to check that the seacock for the raw-water cooling system is open and that the raw-water strainer is not blocked.

THE AUXILIARY ENGINE

Sailors got along just fine for thousands of years without engines. Knowing they were always at the mercy of wind and currents, they planned every maneuver with great care. When the wind died completely, they resorted to oars. Large sailing ships would be towed by crews of oarsmen in the ship's boats. Steam engines came on the scene in the early 19th century, but few yachts had the benefit of auxiliary engines until the development of compact internal combustion engines in the 20th century.

Today, the engine is an integral part of a cruising sailboat. It enables us to maneuver the boat in tight situations and in adverse conditions, such as contrary winds and currents, that would thwart us under sail. The engine also generates electricity for charging batteries, which in turn power the equipment and amenities that enhance safety and comfort for all aboard.

Establish a routine for checking the readiness of the sails and other equipment on board and follow it every time you take the boat out.

On many boats, the engine's gearshift and throttle controls are mounted on the steering pedestal.

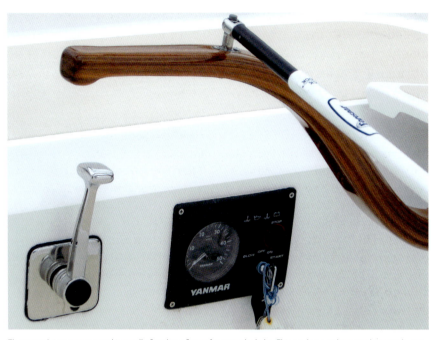

The engine's instrument panel is usually fitted to a flat surface near the helm. This one has a tachometer, key switch, stop button, and warning lights for engine systems.

STARTING PROCEDURE FOR A DIESEL ENGINE

① Turn the battery switch to "Both."

② Move the gearshift back and forth to ensure it's in neutral.

③ Open the throttle (by pushing it forward) to the recommended start setting (usually about 1/4 throttle). Check that the gearshift is still in neutral.

④ Turn the key to "on." A buzzer will sound. This indicates low oil pressure and will turn off once the engine is running.

TIP *If the buzzer continues after the engine has started, or if it sounds after the engine has been running for a while, it indicates either low oil pressure or overheating. Shut the engine down as soon as you safely can and take steps to secure the boat's immediate safety before investigating the problem.*

⑤ A diesel engine usually has a glow plug to preheat a cylinder and facilitate starting. Activate its switch for about 20 seconds.

⑥ Press the start button. An electric starter motor will turn the engine over (just as in a car). Release the start button as soon as the engine starts. Don't crank the engine for longer than 10 seconds at a time so as not to overstress the starter — and the battery.

⑦ Once the engine starts, let it run for a few seconds just to be sure it's running well, then throttle back to idle.

⑧ Check the exhaust outlet (it's usually in the transom). Water should be coming out (it usually does so in spurts.) If none is, shut the engine down immediately. The water in the exhaust is crucial to the engine cooling system (see Chapter 3), and when it doesn't flow, there is a fault in the system that must be addressed.

⑨ Let the engine warm up in neutral at idle speed while you prepare the boat for departure.

This is a good time to step belowdecks for a quick last look around and also to listen to the engine.

TIP *Before putting the engine in gear, check all round outside the boat to make sure no lines have fallen in the water. Nothing will stop an engine faster than a rope wrapped around the propeller shaft. Never let lines trail over the side.*

STOPPING A DIESEL ENGINE

A diesel engine does not require a spark to ignite combustion, so you can't stop it by simply turning off the electricity supply with the key. The stop control on a diesel engine shuts off the fuel supply.

The stop control might be activated electrically with a button or manually by pulling on a T-shaped knob on the control panel.

To stop the engine, bring back the throttle to idle and activate the stop control. As soon as the engine stops, the low-oil-pressure buzzer will sound. You can then switch off the key.

POWER AT YOUR FINGERTIPS

You can use the power of the engine to help you maneuver off a dock in a variety of wind and current conditions. However, to be able to use it safely and to your best advantage, you need to get a feel for just how powerful the engine is and how to control that power. We'll assume that your instructor will handle your first departure (with your help) and will take the boat to a suitable location in calm water free of obstructions and traffic and give you some practice drills.

MANEUVERING UNDER POWER

Driving a sailboat with just the engine is pretty straightforward when you're going in a straight line at a steady speed. It's when you have to turn the boat in a narrow space or bring it gently into a berth that you discover how the boat's momentum, the forces of nature (wind and current), and the idiosyncracies of the propeller affect how you conduct your maneuvers.

MOTORING AT A STEADY SPEED

After your instructor has driven the boat to a suitably unobstructed area and has it motoring forward at a moderate speed, you might be given the wheel, along with the instruction, "Keep her going in a straight line."

As soon as you take hold of the wheel, you might feel a slight vibration. That's the wash from the propeller flowing past the rudder.

Pick a landmark ahead and steer toward it (use the top-dead-center mark on the wheel as a guide). Steer the boat with the wheel as you would a car, making small adjustments to the helm as you need to.

After steering in a straight line for a while, pick a mark on your starboard beam (or port beam, whichever side you have more room) and turn the boat in a wide arc until you are pointing toward your new mark. As you turn, try moving the helm different amounts (but not too far!) to see how that affects the tightness

of your turn. Steady the boat up on your new course.

Next, turn the boat the other way and resume your original course.

SPEEDING UP

As you motor at a steady speed, look at the tachometer on the engine instrument panel and note the rpm at which the engine is running.

Because the engine has only one forward gear, the tachometer is a surrogate speedometer. In calm conditions, the boat will always move at the same speed at the same engine rpm (assuming the boat's bottom and propeller are clean).

While holding the wheel steady, gently move the throttle forward until the tach reading has increased by 500 rpm.

As you continue to steer in a straight line, watch the water alongside (and the speedometer if the boat has one) and note the increase in speed. Note, too, that the boat is more sensitive to the helm.

TIP At full throttle in forward gear, the engine rpm would rise to a maximum and no higher. Normally, you wouldn't operate at maximum rpm because by backing off you'll go almost as fast while the engine burns less fuel and makes much less noise. Most boats have a "sweet spot" on the tachometer where the boat moves at a satisfactory speed with a minimum of vibration from the engine.

SLOWING DOWN

Ease the throttle all the way back to idle, pause while the engine (and prop) slow down, then put the gearshift in neutral. What happened to your boat's speed? Not much, at least for a while.

Sailboats, by design, slip through the water with little resistance. A 30-foot boat can weigh as much as five tons and will carry its way for quite a long distance, especially with no sails up. Even with the help of the engine in reverse gear, it takes time (and distance) to bring a big heavy boat to a stop.

STOPPING THE BOAT WITH THE ENGINE

In an emergency, you can stop a modern sailboat within a couple of boat lengths, but that puts a lot of stress on the propeller and machinery. In normal situations, use the power of the engine judiciously to bring the boat to a stop from a steady speed.

① Gently pull the throttle back so the engine is idling.
② Put the gearshift in neutral.
③ Wait a few seconds for the propeller to slow down, then ease the gearshift into reverse.
④ Slowly increase rpm to give the propeller more bite. Hold the wheel firmly — you will feel some vibration.
⑤ Watch the water next to the boat to assess the boat's speed and ease back on the throttle as the boat comes to a stop.

⑥ As soon as the boat is no longer moving forward, put the throttle in idle and the gearshift in neutral.

TIP Always shift gears slowly and with the engine at idle. Whipping through from full ahead to full astern is a surefire way to cause serious damage in the drivetrain (transmission, propeller, and shaft) that will sooner or later leave you without the use of the engine and with a big repair bill.

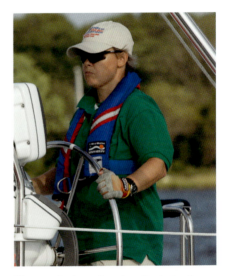

When motoring, keep a firm grip on the wheel so the propeller's wash doesn't deflect the rudder.

THE PROPELLER

As a boat's propeller turns, driven by the engine, it pulls itself through the water in the same way a screw turned by a screwdriver pulls itself into wood. For this reason, a boat's propeller is also called a screw — a boat that has two engines, as many powerboats do, has twin screws. The propeller is fixed to the boat so, as it pulls itself through the water, it takes the boat with it, but it also has some other effects.

PROP WASH

Water isn't solid like wood so, at the same time as the propeller pulls, it also pushes water in the opposite direction — it creates *prop wash*. On most boats, the propeller is forward of the rudder. When motoring forward, the prop wash flows across the rudder and you feel it through the helm. You can turn prop wash to your advantage when maneuvering.

PROP WASH IN ACTION

When the boat is at a standstill, turning the steering wheel produces the same result as turning the steering wheel in a parked car. The engine changes everything.

With the boat stopped, turn the wheel hard to starboard. Put the engine in forward gear and give it about a quarter throttle. Before the boat even begins to move forward, it will turn to starboard.

Now turn the wheel the other way — the boat turns to port.

The boat responds to the rudder as if it were moving forward. That's because the prop wash is pushing against the rudder and, by pushing the rudder to one side, it causes the boat to turn.

PROP WALK

Because prop wash is created by a rotating propeller, it doesn't flow in a straight line but has rotational movement too. This rotation has an effect on the boat called *prop walk*: It tends to "walk" the stern of the boat sideways.

PROP WALK IN ACTION

To see the effect of prop walk, start with the rudder amidships and the boat stopped in the water. Ideally, you'll want calm conditions. If there's wind, begin

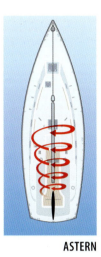

ASTERN

FORWARD

The propeller acts like a screw, pulling the boat through the water and pushing water in the opposite direction.

this exercise with the boat head to wind.

Pick a mark on the shore dead ahead and, while holding the helm firmly amidships, ease the gearshift into forward and nudge the throttle up. Watch the bow against your mark as the prop begins to bite. The bow moves to one side of the mark. This is because prop walk is causing the boat to rotate.

Bring the boat to a stop again. While still keeping the rudder amidships, shift into reverse gear (following the slow and steady rule for shifting gears) and give the engine a little throttle.

This time, the bow moves in the opposite direction — because the prop is rotating in the opposite direction — and more dramatically. Turning the wheel has no effect because the prop wash is flowing forward and not over the rudder.

Prop walk is not very noticeable in forward gear and you can correct for it easily using the prop wash on the rudder.

In reverse it's a different matter. It varies from boat to boat, depending on the location of the propeller, the type of rudder, and other factors, but some boats exhibit pronounced prop walk. At the earliest opportunity, test how prop walk affects your boat because it will dictate how you can maneuver it in close quarters, such as around docks.

PROPELLER "HAND" AND PROP WALK

Prop walk is related to the direction a propeller turns.

A propeller is designated right-handed or left-handed according to which way it turns, as viewed from astern, in forward gear. A right-handed prop turns clockwise and a left-handed prop turns counterclockwise.

Prop walk moves the stern of the boat in the direction the propeller's blades are moving at the **top** of their rotation. On a boat fitted with a right-handed propeller (and that's most sailboats), the stern will walk to starboard in forward gear and to port in astern.

Knowing which way the prop will walk your boat is crucial when you are planning your arrivals at docks (and sometimes your departures).

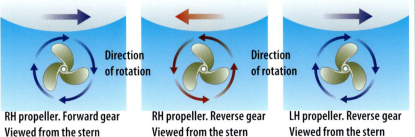

Stern moves to right (starboard)   Stern moves to left (port)   Stern moves to right (starboard)

Direction of rotation   Direction of rotation

RH propeller. Forward gear
Viewed from the stern

RH propeller. Reverse gear
Viewed from the stern

LH propeller. Reverse gear
Viewed from the stern

TIP *On a boat that has no mainsheet traveler, the boom vang is your go-to tool for adjusting twist on all points of sail except close-hauled.*

The farther off the wind you sail, and the more you ease the jibsheet, the more pronounced the twist in the jib becomes. At some point, the top of the sail will be luffing while the foot is overtrimmed.

BROAD REACH

On a broad reach, your sails are no longer working as airfoils; all you really need is a couple of big bags (but nicely shaped big bags) to trap as much wind as you need. Twist is now working against you.

If you let the boom rise and the head of the sail twist off, the upper part of the mainsail will lie on the leeward rigging and spreaders especially if the spreaders are angled aft. Over time, this might result in chafe damage to the sail. Although this is not ideal trim in light winds, with the boom vanged down hard, you'll be able to ease the sail out

farther before this happens. Flattening the sail in this way in stronger winds will also reduce weather helm.

With the jib, the ideal way to reduce twist is to move the jibsheet lead outboard. On many boats, this is not feasible, but moving the lead forward will have a similar effect.

RUNNING

When running, ease the mainsail as far as you can without letting the boom or sails chafe on the standing rigging. If the spreaders on the mast are angled aft, you can't ease the sail any farther out than when broad reaching.

To fly the jib at all, you have to bring it to windward and sail wing-on-wing. How well it sets depends on a number of factors, from the strength of the wind and the size of the waves to the skill of the helmsman. Find its sweet spot by trying different combinations of lead positions and jibsheet tension.

RUN

The Chinese, who invented the full-battened sail, controlled each batten with its own lines. This rig is well suited to running.

BROAD REACH

This boat is barreling along nicely on the edge of a broad reach with a little twist in both mainsail and jib.

ADJUSTING THE JIBSHEET LEAD

Twist in the jib is controlled by the position of the jibsheet lead. Moving the lead forward takes out twist by pulling down on the leech, moving it aft adds twist.

The jibsheet leads through a pulley that's attached to a car. The car is on a track, often called a genoa track, that extends for several feet along the boat's sidedeck.

Unless the car is controlled by a block and tackle, you can only move the car when the sheet is slack, or nearly so. On many boats, the car is held in position by a pin that engages a hole in the track, which is perforated every few inches. Sometimes, the holes are numbered, which gives you a reference when you want to repeat a sail-trim setting.

The best and safest way to adjust the lead on the working jibsheet is as follows:
Estimate where the car needs to be on the track.
Tack the boat.
Go along the now "high" sidedeck (taking the usual precautions).
Move the car to its new position.
Tack back to your original course.
Alternatively, you could take the load off the working jibsheet by using a temporary sheet, or *short sheet* (see page 161). However, this would entail going to the leeward sidedeck, which you should avoid doing whenever possible.

REEFING UNDER WAY

Because you normally reef as a result of an increase in wind strength, possibly accompanied by an increase in the size of the waves, you will sometimes have to do it under some duress. Best, then, to practice the procedure under benign conditions when you can concentrate on mastering the steps involved without having to deal with the stress.

SLAB REEFING

Our mainsail, as on most sailboats with conventional mainsails, has slab reefing. To reef it, we lower it partway and secure it with a new tack and new clew, which are provided by cringles (eyes) pressed and/or sewn into reinforced areas of the luff and leech of the sail.

The reefing clew is controlled by a reefing line, one end of which is attached to the aft end of the boom. The other end leads up through the reefing clew, down to a sheave at the aft end of the boom, then forward inside the boom to the gooseneck. Since our boat is rigged so we can reef the sail from the cockpit, the clew line continues from the gooseneck through a series of blocks and back to a clutch at the cabintop workstation.

A tack reefing line leads in a similar way from the gooseneck, through the reefing tack, and back to another clutch.

On some boats, the reefing tack attaches to a hook on the boom. That means fewer reefing lines in the cockpit but requires someone to work at the mast.

REEFING THE MAINSAIL

On our boat there is no need to leave the cockpit to reef. However, as you have only two winches for the halyard, mainsheet, reefing lines, and topping lift, you need to plan the procedure carefully.

Fake out the tail of the main halyard so it will run freely when you ease it.

Identify the reefing lines for the first reef and see which winch you will use for each of them. Do the same with the boom topping lift.

While reefing, you need the mainsail to be luffing, but you must keep the boat moving so you have steerage. If the boat stops and is then blown off downwind, the mainsail will fill and you'll have difficulty.

The jib can keep you moving on course, but the boat will slow down and the feel of the helm will change noticeably.

While reefing, you will have limited ability to maneuver, so take a good look around to make sure you have clear water.

① Bring the boat to a close reach.

② Ease the mainsheet and the vang.

③ Take up on the boom topping lift (if the boat has one) and make it fast.

....

TIP *The topping lift is important: It will be holding up the boom from the time the halyard is eased until the sail is set and drawing again.*

....

④ Take three or four turns around the winch with the main halyard and grind it in a fraction to unload its clutch.

⑤ Open the clutch and slowly ease the halyard, using the winch as a snubber. As the sail comes down, take up the slack in the tack reefing line.

⑥ Haul the tack reefing line by hand until the new tack is level with the gooseneck. Close its clutch.

⑦ Take up on the halyard until the mainsail's luff is taut and close its clutch.

⑧ **Only then**, haul in the slack in the clew reefing line, then put it on the winch and grind until the clew reef cringle is all the way down to the boom. Make sure the vang is slack while you do this. Lock the reefing line in its clutch.

⑨ Ease the topping lift. As you resume your course, trim the mainsheet and reset the vang.

⑩ Tidy up all the tails: halyard, reefing lines, topping lift, and vang.

....

TIP *Many cruising sailboats have a crew of two, so practice reefing with one person handling the lines while another steers.*

....

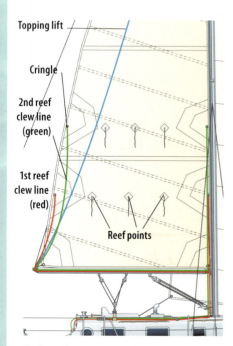

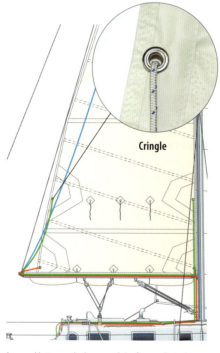

Topping lift
Cringle
2nd reef clew line (green)
1st reef clew line (red)
Reef points
Cringle

The first reef reduces the area of the mainsail by the amount in the panel between the boom and the first-reef cringles. When the reef is taken in, the mainsail fills much less of the triangle between the mast, backstay, and boom. Mainsails commonly have two, sometimes three, sets of reef points, each reducing the area of sail set by about 20 to 25 percent.

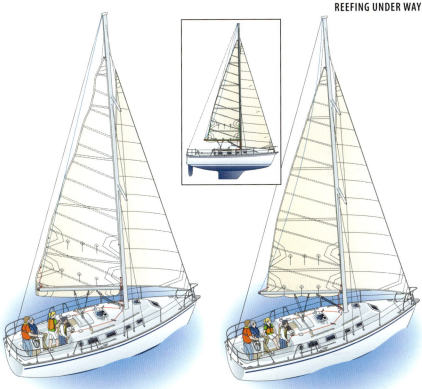

With the boat close reaching under the jib and the mainsail luffing, the main halyard is eased.

After the reef tack has been hauled down and the halyard retightened, the reef clew is hauled down to the boom.

Under way again, the mainsail, now markedly smaller than before, is trimmed as usual with its sheet.

REEFING THE JIB

With roller reefing, taking in a reef in the jib is simply a matter of rolling up some of the sail, but you can take a couple of precautions to ensure the procedure goes smoothly and to protect the sail from potential damage.

If you're sailing on the wind when you decide it's time to reef, don't simply ease the sheet so as to try to roll up some sail. If you do, you'll have to let the sail flog. That's not good for the sail or the boat. A flogging jib can suffer damage and its flailing sheets can damage the boat and inflict a nasty bruise on a person.

Make it easier on the boat, the sail, and the crew by turning downwind to a very broad reach. Once the jib is blanketed behind the mainsail, you can roll it up with little effort. While keeping some tension on the sheet to ensure a tidy furl, take in on the furling line (you might have to use a winch — but carefully!) until you've rolled up enough sail, then make the furling line fast so it can't run out and undo all your work.

But . . . before you turn the boat back to its previous course and trim the jib, you have one more thing to do. Remember the jibsheet car on the track?

That was positioned for trimming the full jib. The "new" sail is shorter along the foot, so the sheet is pulling more along the foot and less on the leech — a recipe for too much twist.

You have to move the car forward. Do this first with the lazy sheet (on the windward side). With luck, the skipper has marked the sail so you roll up a measured amount and has marks on the jibsheet track for the corresponding car position. Next time you tack, adjust the jibsheet lead on the new lazy sheet.

REEFING THE OLD WAY

On some boats, the halyards and reefing lines are not led to the cockpit. To take a reef in the mainsail, someone has to go forward to the mast to work the halyard and set the new tack and clew. To work safely at the mast, that crew needs to be on the high (windward) side of the boat. This means the boat may have to tack before work begins on taking in the reef.

Some boats have jibs that are attached to the forestay with hanks. To reduce sail area, the jib must be dropped and a smaller one hoisted in its place, which requires crew to go to the foredeck to unhank one sail and hank on the new one.

SAFETY TIP *When it's time to reef, anyone going forward should be wearing a safety harness and tether and a life jacket. An inflatable PFD with a built-in harness is ideal for this kind of work.*

When reefing at the mast, it's safest to be "clipped in" and on the windward side of the boat.

SAILING IN SPECIAL SITUATIONS

There will be times when you are unable, or don't wish, to continue sailing in the "normal" way. You have too much wind, or too little wind, or you want to stop for lunch or to wait while friends on another boat catch up. With sails and an engine at your disposal, you have lots of options for handling these situations.

HEAVING-TO

A classic reason to heave-to is to ride out heavy weather at sea. You are unlikely to have to do this at the ASA103 level of cruising, but heaving-to is a fundamental tactic that every seafarer should know as it's useful in many situations. You can delay your arrival at a port until light or tide conditions are favorable; you can "park" the boat while you attend to a repair. When hove-to, a sailboat will lie with the wind forward of the beam while drifting slowly sideways and a little bit forward. The wind on the sails will hold it at a steady angle of heel and the motion, even in big seas, will be relatively easy.

To heave-to, you set the sails in opposition so the jib wants to turn the boat one way and the mainsail the other. You use the rudder to adjudicate.

① Note the wind direction and decide what direction you want to drift: do you want to be on port or starboard tack?

② To lie on the tack opposite to the one you are presently on, sheet the jib in tight, tack, and leave the jibsheet cleated.

③ As the boat passes through head-to-wind, the jib, held by the windward sheet, will set aback and push the bow downwind. Hold the mainsheet on the winch with its clutch open.

④ Steer the boat back toward the wind and make adjustments with the helm and the mainsheet until the boat is lying at a steady attitude to the wind on a close-reaching heading. Normally, the wheel would be turned to windward. The mainsail might or might not need to be luffing.

⑤ Lash the wheel so it can't move (but in such a way you can unlash it quickly).

⑥ Adjust the sheets and helm as needed to maintain the boat's attitude — and keep a sharp lookout.

TIP *If you want to heave-to on the tack you are currently sailing on, the easiest way to do it is to tack twice, rather than trying to haul the jib to windward.*

With the mainsail and jib working in opposition, a boat will lie hove-to almost indefinitely.

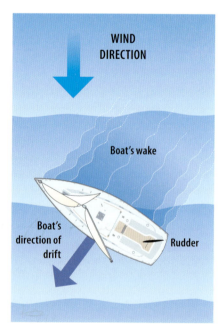

WIND DIRECTION

Boat's wake

Boat's direction of drift

Rudder

Its sail plan and the design of its keel and rudder all affect how any particular boat will heave-to. With the right combination of sail area in the jib and mainsail, most boats will heave-to comfortably even in a moderate gale.

FORE-REACHING

A heavy-weather tactic you can employ that allows you to make slow progress toward a destination to windward is fore-reaching. To do this, furl the jib and continue under mainsail alone, with one or two reefs tied in depending on the wind strength. Sailing the boat as if on a close reach, you'll make a little forward speed but without slipping to leeward as much as when hove-to.

MOTORSAILING

At times, by using the engine and the sails together, you can ensure your day of sailing ends without tension.

Say your home port is tantalizingly close but dead to windward. Sailing would be fun, but it will take too long and you'll arrive after dark, which you don't want to do at this level. Simply motoring straight into the dying wind and leftover waves will be uncomfortable, and possibly wet. This is a time for motorsailing.

When motorsailing to windward, you need only the mainsail set. Sheet it tight with the traveler centered and steer the boat so the sail is just full and drawing. Depending on the boat, the wind speed, and the shape of the sail, you might find you can steer as close as 20 degrees to the apparent wind. Adjust the engine revolutions until you find a speed that affords comfortable progress toward your destination. Even if you have to tack, you will still make better time than if you were just sailing, and the sail will act as a stabilizer in choppy seas.

Avoid motoring into the eye of the wind (or in no wind) with a sail set. The sail will simply flog, which slows the boat down and damages the sail.

In light winds, you may also be able to use the jib, as long as it doesn't luff. The constant thrust from the propeller, even at low rpm, will help you maintain a higher speed than with the sails alone.

Obviously, sailing is more fun, but

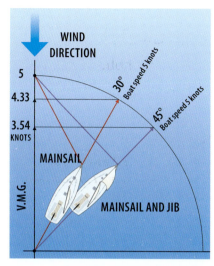

Velocity made good (VMG) is the velocity you are making toward your destination. When you are heading directly toward your destination, your VMG is your speed over the ground (SOG) — where there is no current, that is your boat speed. At the same SOG, your VMG declines as your steered course diverges from your desired course.

motorsailing gives you another tool in the safety toolbox.

LEE SHORE

No collection of sailors' yarns told around a rum bottle on a dark and stormy night would be complete without a lee shore showing up as the villain. Think of Lon Chaney playing the role in the movie version. It doesn't strike such morbid fear into sailors on modern yachts that can sail close to the wind, but on a square rigger, being caught off a lee shore was often a death sentence.

A lee shore can be any obstruction or hazard, from a continent to a fishing pier, toward which the wind

is blowing. On any vessel, the wary skipper avoids getting into a situation that could put him within the grasp of such a threat, and it can have a long reach. It only takes one small thing to go wrong and the boat is that much closer to danger.

When trying to sail away from a lee shore, the psychological tendency is to pinch (sail too close to the wind) which slows the boat down. When you try to tack, you might not have enough headway and end up in irons or, in the stress of the situation, get

an override on a winch. By the time you're sailing again, you are that much closer to the hazard.

In heavy weather, a cruising sailboat is not as closewinded as in medium winds. Add the effects of big seas and a wind-driven surface current, and the problem compounds rapidly.

The prudent skipper carries a mental image of his surroundings and the likely effects of a change in the wind or current and gives potentially hazardous areas as wide a berth as possible.

REVIEW QUESTIONS (see page 176 for answers)

FILL IN THE BLANK OR MATCH THE LETTER WITH THE WORD

1 The ___*skip*___ has ultimate responsibility for the safety of the ___*boat*___ , ___*crew*___ , and passengers.

2 A safety ___*tether*___ may be made of webbing or line and has a clip on either end. One end commonly attaches to a safety ___*harness*___ worn by the crew, the other end is secured to a strong pad-eye or ___*jackline*___ .

3 It is advisable to wear a life jacket in the following situations (name at least three): _____, _____, _____.
  1) Can't swim
  2) Weather *Cold water.*

4 Other than the federally required items, ASA recommends the following additional equipment be carried on board (name at least 10): *radio, cell, rope, chart, and a spare* *fire aid kit, knife, flashlight, tool kit, hand, jar.*

5 The amount of oil in the auxiliary _____ may be checked by withdrawing the _____, wiping it clean, then reinserting and removing again to check the level.

6 The raw-water _____ helps prevent grass, seaweed, and other undesirable debris from entering the engine's _____ system.

7 To help prevent diesel fuel spills, it is better to fill the tank ___*slow*___.

8 It is illegal to dump ___*d*___ anywhere in the ocean or inland waters.

a Plastic

b Engine Oil

c Diesel Fuel

d All of the above

9 Small items of food waste, paper, and glass may legally be discharged if the vessel is more than ___*3*___ miles offshore.

10 Most water-heater appliances have two ways of heating water: either from the engine's _____ system or from _____ electricity.

11 A marine toilet must be connected to a _____ _____ device, which on most boats is a _____ tank.

12 Ways to reduce weather helm and excessive heeling include: (name at least three): _____, *ballast* _____, _____. ~~*bearing*~~, *easing sail – heady up , reefing, traveller*

13 Tightening the *outhaul* decreases the *draft* or "belly" of the mainsail.

14 One way twist in the jib can be adjusted is with the position of the jibsheet car. If the jib has too much twist, move the car ___*aft*___. If it needs more twist, move the car ~~*forward*~~.

15 When reefing the mainsail while under way, it is better to keep the boat moving on a ___*close*___ ___*reach*___ point of sail.
  Close reach to Reef

16 When reefing the mainsail, once the new ___1___ is established, take up the ___2___ again until the luff is tight, then establish the new ___3___.

a Halyard

b Tack

c Clew

17 It is easier to reef or furl the roller-furling jib while on a _____ _____ point of sail.

18 Once the jib is reefed, the jibsheet car (if equipped) should be moved _____ to maintain balanced tension in the leech and foot.

19 When heaving-to, the back-winded ___1___ and leeward-positioned ___2___ are in opposition, causing the boat to sail very slowly with the wind just forward of the ___3___. When a sailboat with wheel steering is hove-to, the wheel would be turned fully to ___4___ .

a Mainsail

b Windward

c Jib

d Beam

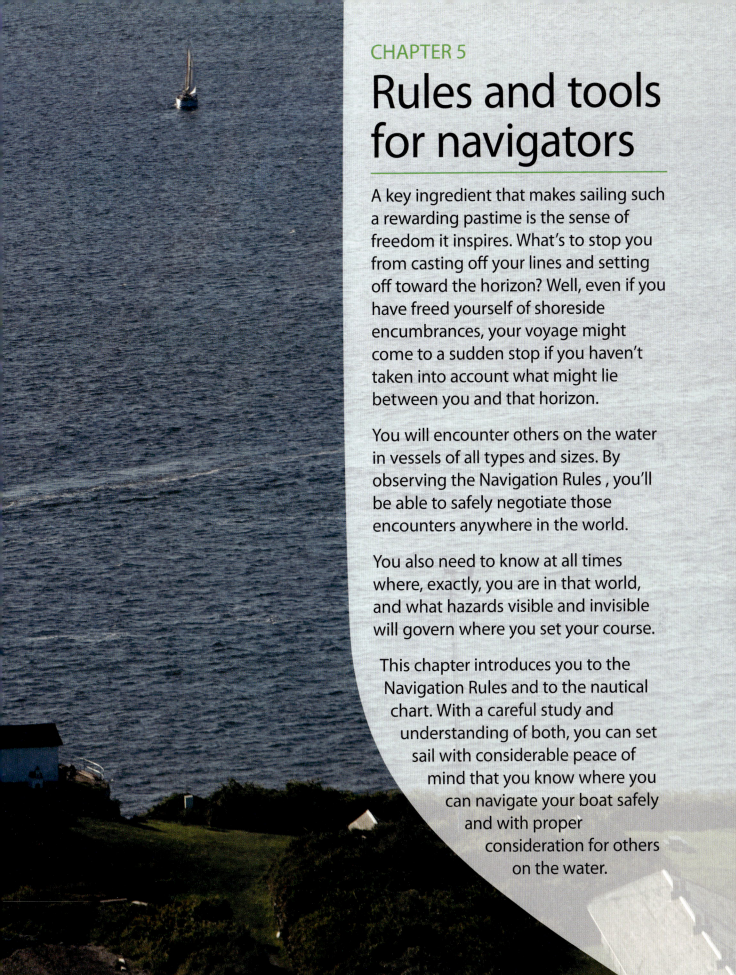

CHAPTER 5

Rules and tools for navigators

A key ingredient that makes sailing such a rewarding pastime is the sense of freedom it inspires. What's to stop you from casting off your lines and setting off toward the horizon? Well, even if you have freed yourself of shoreside encumbrances, your voyage might come to a sudden stop if you haven't taken into account what might lie between you and that horizon.

You will encounter others on the water in vessels of all types and sizes. By observing the Navigation Rules , you'll be able to safely negotiate those encounters anywhere in the world.

You also need to know at all times where, exactly, you are in that world, and what hazards visible and invisible will govern where you set your course.

This chapter introduces you to the Navigation Rules and to the nautical chart. With a careful study and understanding of both, you can set sail with considerable peace of mind that you know where you can navigate your boat safely and with proper consideration for others on the water.

THE NAVIGATION RULES

Oceans and waterways are not like roads and highways, which keep vehicles on fixed routes and instruct their drivers with signs. Boats can travel anywhere there's enough depth to float them and in any direction. Obviously, they need rules to follow if they are to avoid collisions.

THE NAVIGATION RULES

Vessels on the "high seas" anywhere in the world are subject to the International Regulations for the Prevention of Collisions at Sea, often abbreviated to "72 COLREGS." Individual countries may have variations on the rules for inland waters, and COLREGS demarcation lines are printed on nautical charts to indicate the boundaries between international and inland waters.

For vessels operating on US Inland Waters, the US Inland Rules apply. The COLREGS demarcation lines cross the entrances to rivers, estuaries, and bays. Chesapeake Bay and San Francisco Bay, for example, are within US Inland Waters.

In the US, the International and US Inland Rules are published side by side in the publication, *Navigation Rules*, which is available in marine stores and online. US regulations require vessels over 12 meters (40 feet) to carry a copy of the Navigation Rules. The Navigation Rules are numbered 1 through 38. For ASA103, the most applicable rules are Rule 1 through Rule 19. They include important definitions and the "Steering and Sailing Rules" and are the same under International and US Inland Rules.

STAND-ON OR GIVE-WAY

When two vessels are likely to approach one another closely, the Navigation Rules establish which one shall take action to avoid risk of a collision. The vessel required to take action is the *give-way* vessel, the other is the *stand-on* vessel.

APPROPRIATE ACTION

If you determine you are the give-way vessel, Rule 16 requires that you take *"early and substantial action to keep well clear"* of the stand-on vessel. Normally, this would entail making a course change significant enough that the stand-on vessel can clearly see you have taken action to keep clear of it.

If you are the stand-on vessel, Rule 17 requires that you maintain your course and speed. However, you are still obliged under Rule 2, sometimes referred to as the "General and Prudential Rule," to take whatever action is necessary to avoid a collision if it appears the give-way vessel is not taking the action required of it under Rule 16. In other words, you can't knowingly steer your boat into a collision just because you have determined you are the stand-on vessel.

RULE 5: THE LOOKOUT RULE

As well as keeping you out of other kinds of trouble, maintaining a good lookout is crucial to your ability to fulfill your obligation to avoid collisions. Rule 5 makes it a legal requirement:

"Every vessel shall at all times maintain a proper lookout by sight and hearing as well as by all means available appropriate in the prevailing circumstances and conditions so as to make a full appraisal of the situation and of the risk of collision."

Anyone who is on deck at any time for any reason can be a lookout. Even passengers should be encouraged to contribute, especially as on a sailboat the sails sometimes obscure a large sector of the surrounding water from the view of the working crew.

Note that the rule says *"sight and hearing,"* which means you must listen, for engines, for example, and for sound signals or voice hails from other vessels.

When a special event draws a crowd of spectators on the water, every crew on every vessel must maintain an extra vigilant lookout and pay close attention to the actions of those around them.

ESTABLISHING STATUS

Rules 12 through 15 describe the various ways in which vessels can converge and establishes which is the stand-on and which is the give-way vessel in each situation. Rule 18 effectively establishes a "hierarchy" in which a vessel's ability to maneuver can determine its status as stand-on or give-way.

To the sailboat, this looks and feels like a close encounter.

RULE 12: SAILING VESSELS

Sailing vessels have their own subset of rules that apply when the situation is not one of overtaking (see rule 13) and the relative maneuverability of the vessels is not an issue. (You won't encounter many sailing vessels engaged in commercial fishing these days but, if you do, keep well clear of it.)

When two sailing vessels converge on opposite tacks, the vessel on starboard tack (with the wind blowing onto its starboard side) is the stand-on vessel and that on port tack is the give-way vessel.

In this instance, the port-tack sailboat should keep well clear of the starboard-tack boat by tacking or bearing away or by slowing down. To comply with Rule 16 (and common courtesy), make your maneuver early so the stand-on vessel understands your intentions.

Under the Navigation Rules, the position of your boat's main boom determines which tack you are on. If the boom is to port, you are on starboard tack, even if you are sailing by the lee.

TIP *If you are the give-way vessel, do not attempt to sail across the bow of the stand-on vessel if there's the least chance you will pass close to it. Until you are clear of it, you are on converging courses, and if anything causes you to slow down, you risk collision. By turning to pass astern, you put the boats on diverging courses.*

When two sailboats on the same tack are approaching one another, the boat to windward is the give-way vessel. The windward boat would most often alter course to pass astern of the stand-on vessel. Again, make your move early and your intentions clear.

Assume nothing. If you are on port tack and are unable to determine on what tack a sailboat approaching from windward is sailing, take action early to keep clear of it.

When its engine is running and in gear, a sailboat is considered a power-driven vessel for the purposes of the Navigation Rules, and Rule 12 does not apply.

RULE 13: OVERTAKING

When one vessel is overtaking another, the overtaking vessel must keep out of the way of the vessel being overtaken.

A common misconception held by people unfamiliar with the Navigation Rules is that power always gives way to sail. That is not the case when overtaking (and in some other situations, as we'll see). Under Rule 13, a sailboat under sail must keep clear when overtaking a power-driven vessel.

A vessel is considered to be overtaking you if it is approaching within an arc between your stern and 22.5 degrees aft of your beam on either side.

While you are being overtaken, maintain your course and speed, as required by Rule 17, until the overtaking vessel is clear ahead.

The overtaking rule also applies before the sail-on-sail rules.

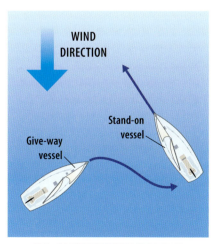

SAIL: PORT TACK/STARBOARD TACK

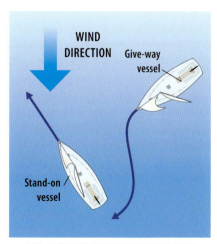

SAIL: LEEWARD/WINDWARD SAME TACK

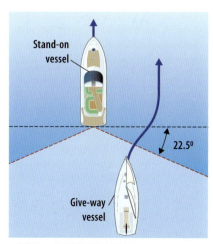

RULE 13: OVERTAKING VESSEL KEEPS CLEAR

RULE 14: HEAD-ON SITUATION

A head-on situation is one in which two power-driven vessels are meeting on virtually reciprocal courses. In such a situation, the rules require both vessels to turn to starboard, so that they pass port side to port side.

TIP *In a narrow channel, this means that traffic keeps to the right-hand, or starboard side of the channel, and is described specifically in Rule 9: Narrow Channels.*

The car carrier is restricted by its draft to navigating in the marked channel. The sailboat is not, and must keep clear.

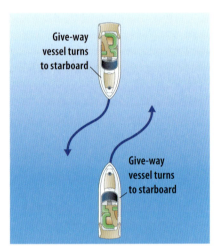

RULE 14: POWERBOATS MEETING

RULE 15: CROSSING SITUATION

If two power-driven vessels are neither meeting nor in an overtaking situation, they are, by definition, crossing.

When two power-driven vessels are

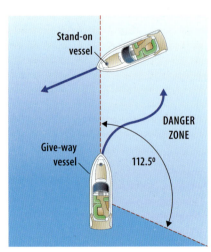

RULE 15: POWERBOATS CROSSING

crossing, the one that has the other vessel on its starboard side gives way.

This rule is so simple because, when crossing, only one boat can be to starboard of the other. Remember, your sailboat becomes a "power-driven vessel" the moment you engage your engine.

VESSELS DRIVEN BY OARS

The Navigation Rules do not mention human-powered vessels such as rowboats or kayaks. Since they are vulnerable, be courteous and give them as wide a berth as possible.

RULE 18: RESPONSIBILITIES BETWEEN VESSELS

This rule makes clear that a sailboat under sail does not have carte blanche "right of way" over the rest of the maritime world. You have to keep a sharp lookout not just so you spot other vessels but also so you can identify them, determine what they are doing, and what they are perhaps incapable of doing. Rule 18 establishes what you might think of as a "hierarchy of privilege" in which vessels able to maneuver freely must give way to vessels less able to maneuver. A vessel in the following list is the give-way vessel in any encounter with a vessel in a category that precedes it.

1 Not Under Command A vessel that is not under command is one that is unable to maneuver because it has lost its propulsion or steering, for example. If you see a vessel that appears to be "not under command," stay clear.

2 Restricted in its Ability to Maneuver The Navigation Rules give specific examples in Rule 3. They include vessels that are connected to the seabed (such as dredges) or engaged in work that prevents them from maneuvering *as required by these Rules.* Such vessels are required to exhibit special shapes (daytime) and lights (nighttime) to advise other vessels of their status.

Use a little discretion. Your medium-sized sailboat would normally be considered well able to maneuver, so be on the lookout for less agile vessels.

If you see a tugboat, for example, look behind it — not just at its stern but as far as half a mile beyond. Tugs are usually towing something, and that something might be a fully laden fuel barge the size of a football field and very low in the water. While the tug may not be considered restricted under Rule 3, even

RULE 9: NARROW CHANNELS

Rule 9 states: "**A vessel less than 20 meters in length or a sailing vessel shall not impede the passage of any other vessel navigating within a narrow channel or fairway.**"
If you are sailing or motoring in or near a marked channel, be on the lookout for larger vessels that may be restricted to navigating within that channel. Even overtaking situations, which are cut and dried in open waters, require cooperation and communication between the overtaking and the overtaken. Don't cross a channel if by so doing you will impede a vessel navigating within the channel.

if you think you are the stand-on vessel, the safest thing to do is to steer clear of any tug and tow. The tug's captain will thank you.

3 Constrained by Draft This part of Rule 18 covers situations not specifically described in Rule 9: Narrow Channels (see box on preceding page). It requires that even when not sailing in a marked channel, you must keep a mental picture of the depths in the vicinity in case a power-driven vessel you might expect would change course to avoid you cannot because doing so would send it into shallow water.

4 Engaged in Fishing Fishing vessels can be identified by their shapes and the gear they carry. A fishing vessel moving slowly might be towing nets. If so, it should be showing day signals (and special lights at night) but even if it's not, stay clear and especially don't sail close astern of it as the gear may be close to the surface.

A sport-fishing boat towing lines is not considered under Rule 18 to be "engaged in fishing" because it is still able to maneuver freely.

5 Under Sail A vessel under sail is required to give way to vessels that might be in any of the above categories, so be

on the lookout for them. In encounters with other sailing vessels, Rule 12 applies.

6 Power Driven A power-driven vessel that is not in any of the above categories must give way to any vessel that is. A sailboat that is motoring, even if it has sails up, is a power-driven vessel.

TIP *The "power gives way to sail" privilege accorded sailing vessels dates from the age when steam and working sail shared the seas. As a recreational vessel, you'll earn the regard of working seafarers if you stay out of their way when you can.*

SECURITY ZONES
The Department of Homeland Security imposes security zones around vessels of the US Navy. No vessel may approach within 100 yards of a naval vessel longer than 100 feet. All vessels within 500 yards of such a naval vessel must operate at the minimum speed necessary to maintain a safe course.

In some areas, security zones are enforced around large commercial vessels and vulnerable structures on the shore. Be on the lookout for guard boats and for buoys marking restricted areas.

QUICK REFERENCE
When there is a risk of collision, no matter how slight, you have to be prepared to take appropriate action, and watch the other vessel for signs of actions it might be taking. Memorize this summary of the rules and you will be prepared for most situations you'll encounter on a day sail.

1	RESTRICTED	Stands On
	MANEUVERABLE	Gives Way
2	OVERTAKEN	Stands On
	OVERTAKING	Gives Way
3	SAIL ONLY	Stands On
	POWER DRIVEN	Gives Way
4	STARBOARD TACK SAIL	Stands On
	PORT TACK SAIL	Gives Way
5	LEEWARD SAIL	Stands On
	WINDWARD SAIL (both on same tack)	Gives Way
6	HEAD-ON (power)	Turn to starboard, to pass port to port.

Select "textbook links" under the "sailing resources" section of www.asa.com for more on the Navigation Rules.

This lobster boat is in the process of hauling pots, so is "engaged in fishing." Learn to identify your local fishing fleet and its activities so you can anticipate the boats' movements.

RULE 10: TRAFFIC SEPARATION SCHEMES

In areas where a large volume of shipping converges, such as at the approaches to major ports, vessels traveling in opposite directions are kept apart by traffic-separation schemes, the maritime equivalent of divided highways. The lanes are marked on charts with dashed magenta lines and the separation zone (the median) is shaded magenta. In some areas, the separation zone is marked on the water with yellow buoys with yellow flashing lights.

A vessel operating in a traffic-separation scheme is required to use the lane designated for its direction of travel. Just as in highway systems in most of the world, traffic keeps to the right, and slower vessels keep to the right-hand side of their lanes.

Vessels must not operate within the separation zone (the median) except when crossing the separation scheme or to avoid danger in an emergency.

Avoid crossing a traffic separation scheme where practicable. If it's unavoidable, Rule 10 requires that you cross at a right angle to it, or as close to that as conditions permit, and as quickly as possible. (Use the engine if necessary.) Do not cause traffic using the scheme to alter course.

Sailboats and other smaller craft are not required to use a separation scheme if an inshore zone is available, and in fact it's best to stay well away from them. If you do have to use one, use the appropriate lane and follow the rules as if you were in a narrow channel — stay to the right of your lane and don't impede traffic that is required by the Navigation Rules to travel in the separation scheme.

....

TIP *Big ships move surprisingly fast and require great distances to stop and even to alter course. If you find yourself in the company of ships, watch them closely and stay out of their way.*

....

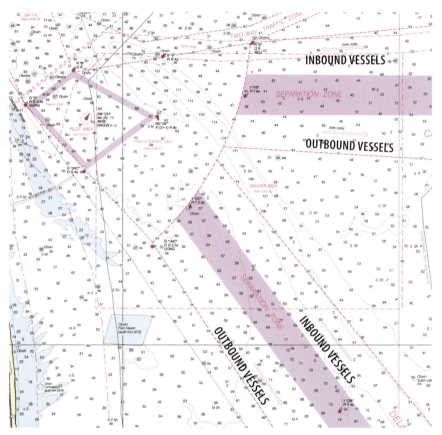

In traffic separation schemes, the areas shaded magenta on the chart serve as "medians" that keep inbound and outbound vessels apart and minimize the number of crossing situations.

Both sailboat and ship are power-driven vessels and must pass port side to port side when in a narrow channel.

MANEUVERING AND WARNING SIGNALS

When vessels are maneuvering in close proximity, it's helpful if they can convey to each other information about the actions they are engaged in or are about to undertake. The Navigation Rules prescribe sound signals for this purpose in Rule 34, but similar signals have different meanings depending on whether they are used in International or US Inland waters.

DANGER SIGNAL

Under both International and US Inland Rules, five short blasts on the whistle signals "I am unsure of your intentions." It's often employed by large vessels to get the attention of smaller craft in busy waters where maneuvering room is limited. If you hear this signal, pay attention, and be prepared to take action. Never put your boat in a situation, such as getting too close to a ship, where the signal might be directed at you.

ACTION SIGNALS

Under both International and US Inland Rules, three short blasts means "I am operating astern propulsion." This does not necessarily mean the vessel is moving backward — it might be trying to stop its forward motion.

Under the International Rules, one short blast means "I am altering course to starboard." Two short blasts means "I am altering course to port."

These two signals have very different meanings under the US Inland Rules.

TIP *The term "whistle" comes from steam whistle — it doesn't sound like the one the soccer coach blows. It might be powered by air or steam, or it can be generated electronically. On our sailboat, the air horn serves the purpose. Mouth-blown horns are also effective.*

SIGNALS OF INTENT

Under the US Inland Rules, whistle signals are required of power-driven vessels in sight of one another and within a half mile of each other when meeting, crossing, or overtaking. These sound signals are used to indicate intent.

One short blast means "I intend to leave you on my port side."

Two short blasts means "I intend to leave you on my starboard side."

The vessel to which the signal is

ONE WHISTLE, TWO WHISTLES

Most commercial vessels use the VHF radio (Channel 13) to communicate "bridge to bridge," and when they do so in Inland waters are not required to use the one-whistle and two-whistle sound signals. On the radio, they use shorthand terms, such as "my one" or "your two," which can be confusing if you don't use them every day. If you engage in these conversations, ask the other skipper to say "my port side" if that's what he means.

directed must reply. If it is in agreement with the signaling vessel, it responds with the same signal. If the responding vessel is not in agreement, it sounds the five-blast danger signal.

Vessels under sail are not required to use these signals of intent. However, sailboats using the Gulf or Atlantic Intracoastal Waterways are powerboats most of the time and their crews need to understand passing signals directed at them and respond to them appropriately.

Composite units, like this pusher tug and barge, are a common sight in estuaries and rivers. In open water, the tug will tow the barge.

SAILING IN REDUCED VISIBILITY

Whenever possible, avoid sailing in conditions of reduced visibility. As when driving in fog, not being able see where you're going or what other vessels are doing adds danger. If it dawns misty, or the weather forecast calls for fog, stay put and wait for things to improve. Be prepared, though, in case the weather clamps down unexpectedly and your world suddenly becomes dim.

WEATHER WISE

Normally, fog, or mist, or even heavy rain, doesn't descend without warning. Although any one of these can envelop you quite quickly, you can usually see signs that it's coming. That's the time — before visibility deteriorates — to use every tool you have to establish your position and the course you will have to steer to bring you to a place of safety.

RADAR REFLECTOR

Fiberglass boats, even those with metal masts, show up poorly on radar, so hoisting a radar reflector aloft increases the chance your boat will appear on the screens of vessels equipped with radar. However, you have to still rely on listening for sound signals and keeping a sharp lookout. In poor visibility, never assume other vessels have seen you.

TIP *Sea fog of the kind that forms when warm moist air meets cold water is usually clearly visible from a distance, lying like a thick cotton blanket on the sea surface. If you can't avoid steering into it, make sure you know where you are and where you should be going before you do.*

SIGHT AND SOUND

Before you lose visibility, use your eyes, the chart, and the navigation tools to establish where you are. Also, try to note the positions and courses of other vessels so they won't surprise you when they loom out of the mist.

When the gloom descends, keep a sharp lookout, operate at a safe speed, make the sound signals prescribed in the Navigation Rules, and listen for sound signals from other vessels.

SOUND SIGNALS

A vessel under 12 meters (40 feet) in length is not "obliged" under the Navigation Rules to produce the sound signals required of larger vessels. However, Rule 35(g) requires that it "make some other efficient sound signal at intervals of not more than 2 minutes."

This is where you use the air horn that's kept with the safety equipment.

The signal required of a vessel under

sail is one prolonged blast followed by two short blasts, repeated at intervals of not more than 2 minutes. This is the same signal sounded by vessels in the "hierarchy" listed on pages 86-87 with the exception of power-driven vessels.

A power-driven vessel under way must sound one prolonged blast at intervals of not more than 2 minutes.

If the wind is light and you choose to use the engine to give you the option of more speed and maneuverability in case you have to take avoiding action, you're sailboat becomes a power-driven vessel and must make the appropriate signal.

In poor visibility, use all your senses — sight, hearing, and even smell — to establish where you are and what you might encounter.

LISTEN

In fog, your best sense is hearing. Sound carries even through fog and, as well as the sound signals of other vessels, you will hear foghorns and the bells and gongs of buoys. For this reason, if you have breeze, it's sometimes better to sail than to run the engine. If you do choose to motor, position someone on the bow, well away from the noise of the engine.

SAFE SPEED

Rule 6 of the Navigation Rules requires every vessel to proceed at a safe speed at all times. In determining that safe speed, vessels must take into account not just visibility but the density and type of traffic and the time and space needed to "*take proper and effective action*" should the need arise.

When motoring, you can change course simply by turning the wheel. Sailing maneuvers take more time to execute.

If everyone is in place, you can tack quite promptly, but a jibe is another matter.

While jibing would not be your preferred course of action, you might not have a choice, especially in poor visibility. Your safe speed, then, is determined by the distance you will cover between the time you decide you must jibe and the time you have completed the jibe and are sailing on your new course.

The faster you are sailing, the wider your "early warning radius" needs to be. If you are sailing at 6 knots and it takes two minutes from the time you first think, "I must jibe" to the time you are on the new jibe, that radius is nearly a quarter mile. Do you have a quarter mile visibility?

NAVIGATION LIGHTS

The Navigation Rules require vessels to display navigation lights between sunset and sunrise and in times of restricted visibility. While you won't be doing any night sailing in ASA103, you could well encounter restricted visibility in a heavy downpour or fog, or you might unintentionally get caught out after sunset when the wind dies. You therefore need to know what lights to display and how to read the lights of vessels around you.

COLORS AND ANGLES

The Navigation Rules prescribe the colors of lights and how they are arranged on different vessels. The lights convey information about a vessel's type, its size, and any activity it is engaged in, such as towing. Defined arcs of visibility allow crew on one vessel to determine another vessel's relative heading.

NOTE The lights described below are to be shown between sunset and sunrise and in times of restricted visibility.

SIDELIGHTS

All vessels under way must display a red light, called a *sidelight*, on the port side and a green sidelight on the starboard side. The arc of visibility of each sidelight is 112.5 degrees — from the bow to 22.5 degrees abaft the beam. If you recall Rule 15 (see page 86), you will note that, in a crossing situation, the vessel that can see the other vessel's red sidelight is the give-way vessel.

STERN LIGHT

All vessels under way must show a white *stern light*. Its arc is 135 degrees — from 22.5 degrees abaft the beam on the starboard side to 22.5 degrees abaft the beam on the port side. This arc of visibility of the stern light is the same arc as the "overtaking zone."

Sailboats under 65 feet (20 meters) may carry the sidelights and stern light in a single lantern at the masthead.

MASTHEAD LIGHT

A power-driven vessel under way must show a white *masthead light* that is visible in the arc covered by the combined red and green sidelights. A power-driven vessel over 164 feet (50 meters) must show two masthead lights, one aft of and higher than the other.

To distinguish it from a power-driven vessel, a vessel under sail does not show a masthead light. However, when motoring, a sailboat must show a masthead light. Often called a steaming light, it's usually mounted on the mast, about halfway up on the forward side.

NOTE A sailboat under 23 feet (7 meters) is not required (but is recommended) to carry the lights described above. A boat not equipped with the lights must have a flashlight to shine on the sails. When that sailboat is motoring, it must display the lights required of a power-driven vessel.

ANCHOR LIGHT

A vessel at anchor is required to display *"an all-round white light where it can best be seen."* Many sailboats are fitted with a light at the masthead that technically meets this requirement but an *anchor light* hung lower down between the mast and the forestay is often more easily seen from boats passing through the anchorage.

Between sunrise and sunset, a vessel at anchor is required to suspend a black ball in the forward part of the vessel.

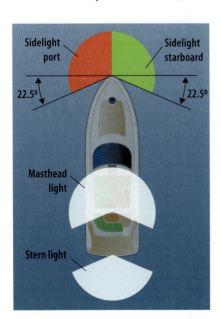

Power-driven vessels under 50 meters show these lights. A sailboat **under sail** does **not** show the masthead light.

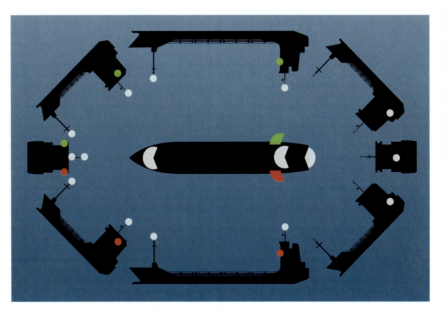

A vessel's navigation lights appear in different patterns from different angles, and indicate the vessel's heading relative to your boat. By rotating the page, you can see how the lights on a ship longer than 50 meters appear from various viewpoints.

AIDS TO NAVIGATION

An experienced navigator with the right charts and tools should be able to negotiate any stretch of water without any aid from outside the boat. In areas where the water is shallow, locating and staying in navigable water demands precision, and the required piloting skills take years to master. But safe navigation is crucial to commerce, so the government provides aids to navigation for the benefit of all shipping.

THE LATERAL SYSTEM

Much of the U.S. Aids to Navigation System (USATONS) is made up of lateral aids — buoys and beacons set along the sides of channels to mark the limit of navigable water. (Lighthouses and other beacons aid in establishing the boat's position but are not part of the lateral system.)

BUOYS AND BEACONS

Buoys float on the water and are anchored to the bottom. Beacons are permanent structures that are most often fixed to the bottom of the body of water but are sometimes installed on land. In the USATONS, red buoys and beacons mark the right-hand side of a channel for vessels entering it from seaward or from open water. They are numbered with even numbers that ascend as the channel leads inland.

Green buoys and beacons mark the left-hand side of a channel as it leads inland and have odd numbers.

Buoys and beacons are further distinguished by their shapes.

Unlighted red buoys are in the form of a cylinder with a conical top — and are called "nuns" because of this shape.

Red-side beacons carry a red triangle.

Unlighted green buoys are straight cylinders and are referred to as cans. Green-side beacons carry a green square.

Some buoys and beacons carry lights that match their color. Red and green lighted buoys are not distinguished by their shapes but are visibly different from unlighted buoys.

REGULATORY MARKERS

Information and Regulatory Markers are white cylindrical buoys with orange stripes above and below one of four shapes.

A diamond shape warns of Danger at that location. A diamond shape with a cross inside indicates an Exclusion Zone (boats keep out).

A circle marks a Controlled Area, such as a speed-limit or no-wake zone.

A rectangle is used to display information such as directions or distances.

DANGER

CONTROLLED AREA

EXCLUSION

INFORMATION

TIP *To remember which side to pass a buoy or beacon, think of the commonly used phrase, "red right returning." When heading home from the sea, or when heading upstream in a river or estuary, leave red marks to your right-hand, or starboard, side.*

Where a channel divides or meets another, the junction is marked with a buoy with red and green horizontal bands. The color of the top and bottom bands, and, if it's lighted, of the light, indicates which side of the preferred channel it marks.

TIP *Nautical charts show the locations of ATONs and their characteristics — color, number, shape, light, etc. Chart No. 1 (see Page 94) explains these notations.*

IALA REGIONS A AND B

Two different lateral systems of buoyage are used around the world. North America uses IALA Region B, in which the "red right returning" rule applies. In IALA Region A, which is much of the rest of the world, among other differences, red marks indicate the left-hand side of a channel when traveling from seaward.

Heading out to sea, the boat is leaving the green can buoy — a lateral mark — to its starboard side. The lighthouse ashore is not a lateral mark but helps the navigator establish the boat's position.

NUN BOUY
with yellow
ICW triangle

CAN BUOY with
yellow ICW
square

**GREEN LIGHTED
BEACON** with
yellow ICW
triangle

**JUNCTION
MARK** marks
red side of
preferred
channel

**RED DAY
BEACON**

**GREEN DAY
BEACON**

**RED LIGHTED
DAY BEACON**

**JUNCTION
MARK** leave to
green side for
preferred channel

**LIGHTED
GREEN BUOY**

**LIGHTED
RED BUOY**

**SAFE WATER
BUOY** pass on
any side

Secondary channel

Preferred channel

Intracoastal
waterway: New Jersey
to Texas

INTRACOASTAL WATERWAY

The Intracoastal Waterway (ICW) provides a largely
inland and protected route along the US Atlantic and
Gulf Coasts from New Jersey to the Mexican border.
For much of its length it follows rivers and estuaries
and shares ATONs laid in the lateral system. Those
shared buoys and beacons are marked with yellow
squares or triangles to identify them as ICW markers.

In many places, the ICW transitions from going
"up" one river to going "down" another, so the
triangles and squares can appear on either red or
green ATONs. When traveling in the direction from
New Jersey to Texas, ATONs marked with yellow
triangles are to be left to starboard and those
marked with yellow squares are to be left to port.

The ATONs depicted are just a few of the many lateral aids employed in US waters. Pay extra attention, especially to the
numbers on the buoys and beacons, where channels meet or diverge. When entering a channel from open water,
remember "red, right, returning" and ascending numbers — even numbers on red ATONs, odd numbers on green.

THE NAUTICAL CHART

Some people are fascinated by maps and, before setting off on any kind of road trip, will study them for hours. Others get by with asking directions. This latter group won't get very far on the water. To go anywhere on the water in safety, you must be aware of everything around you both above and below the water. And because you can't see what lies beneath the water, you need a map to show you what's there. That map, the nautical chart, also provides much more information essential to safe navigation.

CHART NO. 1

Every map needs a legend that explains the meanings of all the symbols and notations found on it. Such a legend on a nautical chart would take up more space than the chart itself, so that legend is published separately.

Charts of US waters are published by the National Oceanographic and Atmospheric Administration (NOAA). NOAA Chart No. 1 illustrates and explains every notation found on a NOAA chart and should be in the library (or hard drive) of every serious sailor. Similar publications are available from agencies that publish nautical charts in other countries.

CHART SOURCES

NOAA charts are available through authorized retailers such as marine stores and specialist bookstores. Some outlets offer "print on demand," a service that ensures the chart you purchase has been corrected by NOAA with information available up to the print date.

The same up-to-date charts are available in electronic form on the NOAA website and can be downloaded for viewing on a computer.

NOAA also supplies data to commercial interests that then repackage it in a number of forms, from charts bound in books to electronic charts for use with electronic navigation instruments. Chart books are convenient for use aboard cruising boats and often include useful supplemental information.

CHART ORIENTATION

Charts, and most maps, are usually drawn with north "up" — north is at the top; south is at the bottom. On the sides of the chart you will see graduations in degrees and minutes of Latitude. Along the top and bottom of the chart you will see graduations in degrees and minutes of Longitude.

CHART DATUMS

For any geographical locations, elevations, or water depths to have meaning, they need reference points. Nautical charts were compiled for centuries by dozens of maritime nations, each with its own set of reference points, or *datum*. Even the location of Longitude Zero was not agreed on globally until 1884.

NOAA charts use the internationally recognized WGS 84 datum for geographic locations.

Of more immediate interest to a sailor in home waters is the datum for *soundings*, the depth of the water. It's printed on the chart, and is usually "mean lower low water." That means that a depth marked on the chart is the depth at a very low state of tide, so except during particularly low tides, that is the least depth you would expect to find at that location.

TIP *A sounding printed on a chart reflects the depth on the the day the survey was made, which might have been 20 or even 100 years ago. Where the seabed is mobile, as in shallow sandy areas, wind, tide, silting, and erosion can cause depths to change. Treat soundings with suspicion.*

CHART NOTES

Nautical charts are usually strewn with notations, such as "Restricted Area, see Note A." Be sure to read them as they may affect how you plan your day sail.

CHART SYMBOLS

For a complete description of chart symbols you'll need a copy of Chart No. 1, but here are a few examples of chart details to get you started. Make sure to read the notes printed around the chart's title plate and along the bottom margin as these provide information on the chart scale, datum, units of measurement for soundings (depths), and the date to which the chart has been corrected.

⊙	Riprap surrounding light
▲ R Bn	Triangular-shaped beacons
■ G Bn	Square-shaped beacons
♦	Lighted marks on standard charts
●	Major light, minor light, light, lighthouse
♦ R "2"	Starboard-hand buoy (entering from seaward - US waters)
♦ "1"	Port-hand buoy (entering from seaward - US waters)
⊕	Dangerous wreck, depth unknown
+++	Sunken wreck, not dangerous to surface navigation
⊿	Wreck showing any portion of hull or superstructure at level of chart datum
⬚	Fish haven (artificial fishing reef)
∿	Submarine cable
S	Sand M Mud G Gravel
Rk; rky	Rock; Rocky
⌒	Area with stones, gravel, or shingle
⌣	Rocky area, which covers and uncovers
⊙R TR	Radio tower ⊙TV TR TV tower
⊙STANDPIPE	Standpipe ⊙CUPOLA Cupola
⊙SPIRE	Spire ⊙WTR TWR Water tower
⊙CHIMNEY	Chimney

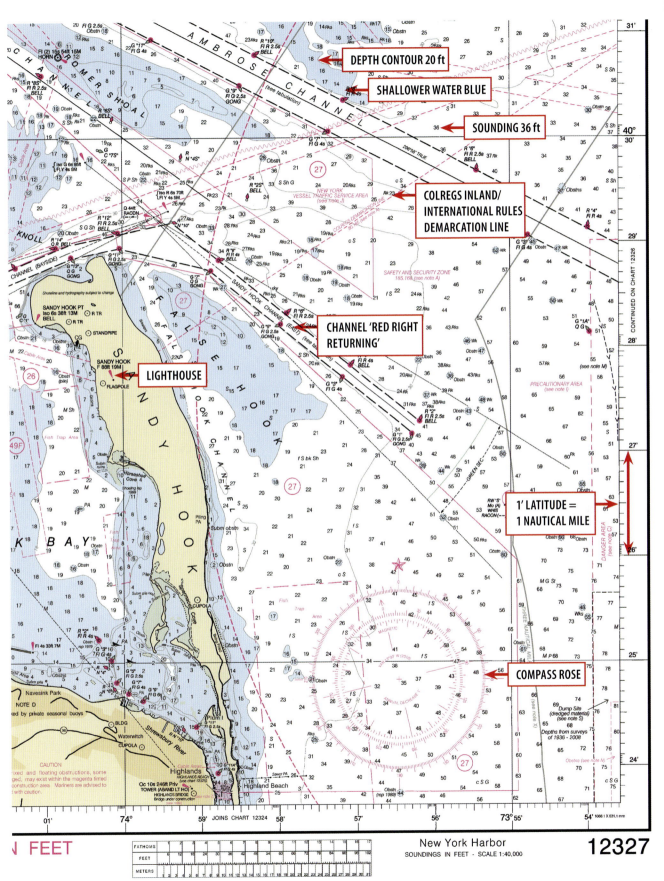

DEPTH CONTOUR 20 ft

SHALLOWER WATER BLUE

SOUNDING 36 ft

COLREGS INLAND/
INTERNATIONAL RULES
DEMARCATION LINE

CHANNEL 'RED RIGHT
RETURNING'

LIGHTHOUSE

1' LATITUDE =
1 NAUTICAL MILE

COMPASS ROSE

FEET

New York Harbor
SOUNDINGS IN FEET - SCALE 1:40,000

12327

This small corner of a NOAA chart shows just how much information these publications provide. A mariner approaching New York Harbor without this chart would be at a loss.

THE SHIP'S COMPASS

All poet John Masefield asked for was a tall ship and a star to steer her by, but he didn't offer any hint of what he would steer to in daytime. Within sight of land, of course, it's possible to steer toward a landmark (or away from one) and maintain a fairly steady course, as long as no current is setting you to one side or the other. In the absence of stars and landmarks, and even in their presence, the sailor's best friend is the ship's compass.

COMPASS TERMS

Earth is surrounded by a magnetic field that is aligned more or less with the axis between the North Pole and the South Pole. A magnet suspended from a thread (or floating on a liquid) will seek to align itself with Earth's magnetic field. The magnet's north pole is so named because it seeks Earth's North Magnetic Pole.

The marine compass works on this very principle, and has evolved into a sophisticated instrument that remains accurate and reliable even in the roughest of conditions at sea.

In a ship's compass, a magnetic needle is attached to a disk, called the *compass card*, Most modern compass cards are marked in degrees. You'll find older compasses marked with the points of the compass (see box) or a combination of both.

The card is supported on a bearing so it rotates freely within the compass bowl, which is filled with a special oil to dampen the card's movement. The needle, and therefore the card, always points toward Magnetic North (or tries to — see Deviation, facing page).

Fixed to the forward side of the compass bowl is a mark. This is the *lubber's line*. The line between the lubber's line and the center of the compass card lies over the centerline of the boat (or is parallel to it if the compass is off the centerline). The degree mark on the compass card adjacent to the lubber's line indicates the direction in which the boat is pointing, or its *heading*. To steer a boat to a compass course, the helmsman aims to keep the lubber's line adjacent to the mark on the compass card that represents the course he wishes to steer.

TIP *Magnets, anything containing iron (except certain high-grade stainless steels), and electric currents affect the compass. A cell phone within one foot of a compass can deflect the compass card by 20 degrees. Avoid placing items that might influence the compass within three feet of the ship's compass, and that includes flashlights, some deck knives, and portable radios — all those things we like to keep close at hand in the cockpit.*

POINTS OF THE COMPASS

A modern compass card is graduated in degrees, but, until the 20th century, most seamen learned to "box the compass" by naming the 32 *points of the compass*.

The cardinal points are N, E, S, and W, each separated by 90 degrees, or a quadrant. Dividing each quadrant equally are the *semi-cardinal points*, NE, SE, SW, and NW. If you want to know the rest of the points, ask a boy scout.

Weather forecasts and reports usually give wind directions by the cardinal and semi-cardinal points of the compass so, as well as north winds and west winds, you read of southwest (SW) winds or northeast (NE) winds.

We name the wind's direction by the point of the compass *from which it's blowing*. A north wind blows from the north. This convention derives from the practice of the mariners of ancient Mediterranean cultures of naming winds according to their source — the mountains, the Levant — which also implied specific characteristics; a south wind brought rain, a west wind was mild, a northeast wind was cold. The winds were depicted in a circular pattern that resembled the petals of a rose — and the pattern persisted in the design of compass cards.

A classic compass card shows points and numbers.

Many modern compass cards retain only the numbers. On this compass, the lubber's line is at 340 degrees.

THE COMPASS AND THE CHART

Before the compass, sailors used a variety of means to establish what direction they were sailing when out of sight of land. At night, like Masefield, they used the stars. But stars are unreliable because they move across the sky. The compass is relatively constant, and a facsimile of a compass card printed on a chart gives a navigator a convenient way to figure courses to steer.

THE COMPASS ROSE

A *compass rose* is printed on every nautical chart. It's usually made up of two concentric circles, both of them graduated in degrees and marked N, E, S, and W. The N on the outer circle points to True North, at the top of the chart. The inner circle is aligned with the *magnetic variation* at the location covered by the chart, and therefore often offset by several degrees from the outer circle.

VARIATION

The Magnetic North Pole, that the compass points toward, is not at the geographic North Pole. The difference between the direction to Magnetic North and that to so-called True North is the *magnetic variation*. Variation varies greatly over the earth's surface. The magnetic pole also wanders over time, so the variation at any one location can also change. The direction and rate at which it changes is noted on the compass rose.

> **TIP** *If you proceed to ASA 105, Coastal Navigation, you'll work with both true and magnetic courses and converting one to the other. For now, the important part of the chart's compass rose is the inner, magnetic, circle that corresponds to the card on the ship's compass.*

DEVIATION

Magnets are not monogamous and the magnetic needle in a compass is led astray by anything with iron in it (such as the engine) and by magnetic fields created by electrical devices. The compass can be adjusted to cancel out most fixed influences and the remaining *deviation*, which can be measured by "swinging the compass," noted on a *deviation card*. Deviation should be figured into the "course to steer," but that's for ASA 105.

Deviation is a characteristic of the boat. A boat's compass can be dangerously

misleading if it has not been swung and adjusted, or if it's not used with reference to its deviation card.

PLOTTING A COURSE

When working on a paper chart you need a pencil, dividers, and a parallel rule (see photo).

① On the chart, find two objects, A and B (buoys are good examples), and trace a straight line between them with a finger.

② If that "route" is clear of obstructions, use the parallel rule and pencil to draw a line from A to B.

③ Lay an edge of the parallel rule along your line and "walk" the rule to where one edge passes across the center of a compass rose.

④ Draw a line along this edge to pass through the center and cross both sides of the inner (magnetic) rose.

⑤ Follow this line from the center of the rose in the direction that represents A to B and note the number of degrees where it crosses the magnetic rose. If the number is 295, your course from A to B is 295 degrees magnetic. (Its reciprocal, 115 degrees, on the opposite side of the rose, would be the course from B to A.)

But for deviation, this would be the compass course to steer from A to B. For now, we'll assume that deviation is insignificant.

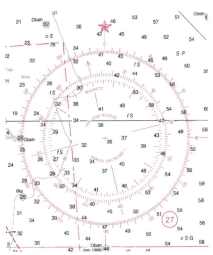

N on the outer circle of the compass rose represents True North, on the inner circle, Magnetic North. The difference, the local variation, is printed at the center (VAR 13°W).

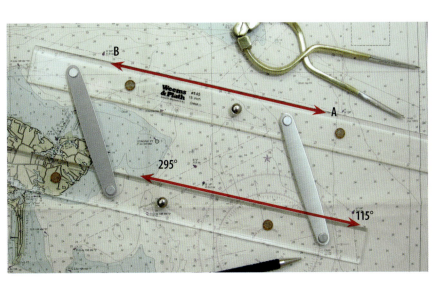

Lay the parallel rule along the planned track and walk it to the inner compass rose to find the magnetic course. Use dividers to measure the distance on the Latitude scale along the side of the chart.

DISTANCE, SPEED, AND TIME

You have a destination and a compass course to steer to bring you there. How long will it take you to get there? If you have laid your course to a buoy, you'll be hard pressed to see that buoy from two miles away, even on a clear day. You need to know when it should be coming into sight.

Use your ASA log book to record your sailing experience and the certificates you have achieved.

DISTANCE

Once you have laid out a safe course to your destination, the next step is to measure the distance you have to sail.

Place one point of the dividers on A and the other on B. Transfer the dividers to a Latitude scale (there's one on each side of the chart). Count the minutes of Latitude betwen the points. This is the distance in nautical miles.

THE NAUTICAL MILE

One nautical mile is the length of one minute of Latitude; one degree of Latitude is 60 nautical miles. A minute of Latitude is the same length everywhere on Earth's surface. Minutes of Longitude become shorter the farther north or south you move from the Equator. Always use Latitude, marked on the left and right margins of the chart, for measuring distances when navigating.

SPEED

Now you know the distance from A to B, estimate how fast you will be sailing, which will depend on the boat and the strength and direction of the wind. Base your estimate on your experience of how fast the boat sails in the expected conditions, and update the result when you see what you are actually achieving when you get under way.

TIME

Divide the distance (in nautical miles) by your estimated speed (in knots) and you have the time (in hours) it should take you to get from A to B. Add that time to your departure time and you have your estimated time of arrival (ETA).

....

TIP *Calculating an estimated time of arrival (ETA) is important when planning a cruise. Do it with best-case and worst-case numbers (think change in the weather), and be prepared to change your plans if the worst case will have you out in conditions (after dark, for example) you're not comfortable handling.*

....

You now have a course and distance to your destination and an estimate of how long it should take you to get there. You need somewhere to write this information down, for immediate use and to refer to next time you want to make the same trip. The place to record this, and other information related to the boat and your adventures aboard it, is in the *ship's log*.

THE SHIP'S LOG

Truck drivers keep logs of their travels — time on the road, mileage, cargo, weight, fuel purchased — and your computer maintains an activity log.

The word log comes from the days of sail, when a ship's speed was calculated by counting the time it took a firewood log thrown off the bow to reach the stern. The numbers obtained were recorded so the navigator could estimate the distance traveled. Other information about the ship's condition, weather, and sea conditions was also recorded in the "log" book, which then became the

official document for the voyage.

Many skippers of cruising sailboats maintain a log for the same reasons ships do. It's the ideal repository for important information about the boat, its crew, and its equipment, the current voyage, and even maintenance schedules and service records for the engine.

Under way, you might note down hourly the boat's position, speed, and course and the weather conditions. You might add notes about anything else of interest, such as any sea life or other vessels you've observed.

Separately from the ship's log, which stays with the vessel, many sailors maintain logbooks for their own personal use and enjoyment. Such a log, if signed by the skippers of the boats on which you sail, can become part of your record of sea time should you ever wish to obtain a mariner's license — and a cherished memento whatever your course through life.

Your ASA Log Book, as the official record of your progress through the ASA certification program, is a valuable part of your sailing résumé. As an ASA member, you can access this record online, which is a great asset when you want to rent or charter a sailboat.

SPEED, DISTANCE, AND TIME

When you know any two of the three factors, speed, distance, and time, you can calculate the unknown one by using one of these equations:

TIME	=	distance/speed
SPEED	=	distance/time
DISTANCE	=	speed x time

ELECTRONIC NAVIGATION

For millennia, sailors navigated almost entirely by eyesight backed up by charts, drawings of coastlines, and tables of information about celestial bodies. They studied everything around them — the sea, the land, the sky, and the creatures that populated them — and used all of those observations to guide them in their travels. They were acutely aware of their surroundings at all times and alert to any hint, through sight, smell, or hearing, of any situation that might put them in peril.

THE GLOBAL POSITIONING SYSTEM

Today, navigators have access to arrays of electronic devices that provide information on everything from the boat's speed to the names of approaching ships, but the innovation that turned navigation from a hard-earned skill to a cell-phone app is the Global Positioning System (GPS).

POSITION

A GPS receiver calculates its position in three-dimensional space by processing signals it receives from an array of orbiting satellites. It is accurate to within feet.

Used in its simplest mode, a GPS on a boat will display the boat's position in latitude and longitude. Using the latitude and longitude scales on the chart's margins, you can plot that position on a chart to confirm (or not) that you are where you think you are. You can then use the elementary navigation procedures described earlier in this chapter to plot a course from that position to where you want to be next.

WAYPOINTS

When giving directions to your house, you might tell your visitors to turn right at the white church and left at the red barn. In the language of

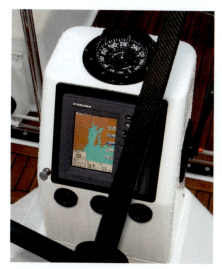

A chart plotter installed on a boat's steering pedestal puts navigation information in front of the helmsman.

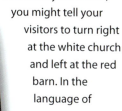

A handheld GPS made for marine use is a handy accessory for a sailor who knows how to navigate.

navigation, the church and barn are waypoints – locations by which you measure progress along the route to your house and at which you might make a change in direction.

You can enter into a GPS the latitude and longitude of any location on the earth's surface. This, too, is a waypoint, and you can save it and give it a name.

When you select a waypoint to "go to," the instrument will display the range (distance from) and bearing (course) to that waypoint from its own location — if it's a handheld device, that's your hand.

ROUTES

You can string waypoints together in the GPS to create a route. Instead of barns and churches, they might be points in navigable water at safe distances from land features or aids to navigation that mark your course. When you call up the route in the GPS, it will give range and bearing to the first waypoint. When you

are approaching the waypoint It will warn you. When you pass it, it will give you range and bearing to the next waypoint in the route.

TIP *Unlike a GPS in an automobile, a marine GPS does not give turn by turn instructions to get you from A to Z. You have to select the waypoints B, C, D, etc., and you have to ensure that, between C and D, for example, there is nothing to interrupt your safe passage — like an island.*

CHART PLOTTER

A chart plotter displays an electronic chart on a screen, and interfaces data from a GPS receiver to locate the boat's position on that chart. You can zoom in or out to view the chart at large scale (close up) or small scale (long range).

The smaller the screen on a chart plotter, the less chart detail it can show. At small scales especially, this often means that crucial information is omitted from the display. Before committing to any course planned on a plotter, zoom in along its entire length to look for potential hazards. Better yet, plot your course on the large-scale paper chart, which will show the critical details.

FUNDAMENTALS FIRST

Learn the underlying procedures for navigating and piloting your boat using the paper chart, the plotting tools (dividers and parallel rule), and your own observations backed up by instruments such as the depthsounder and speed log (speedometer). You can then apply those principles to use electronic navigation instruments safely and effectively.

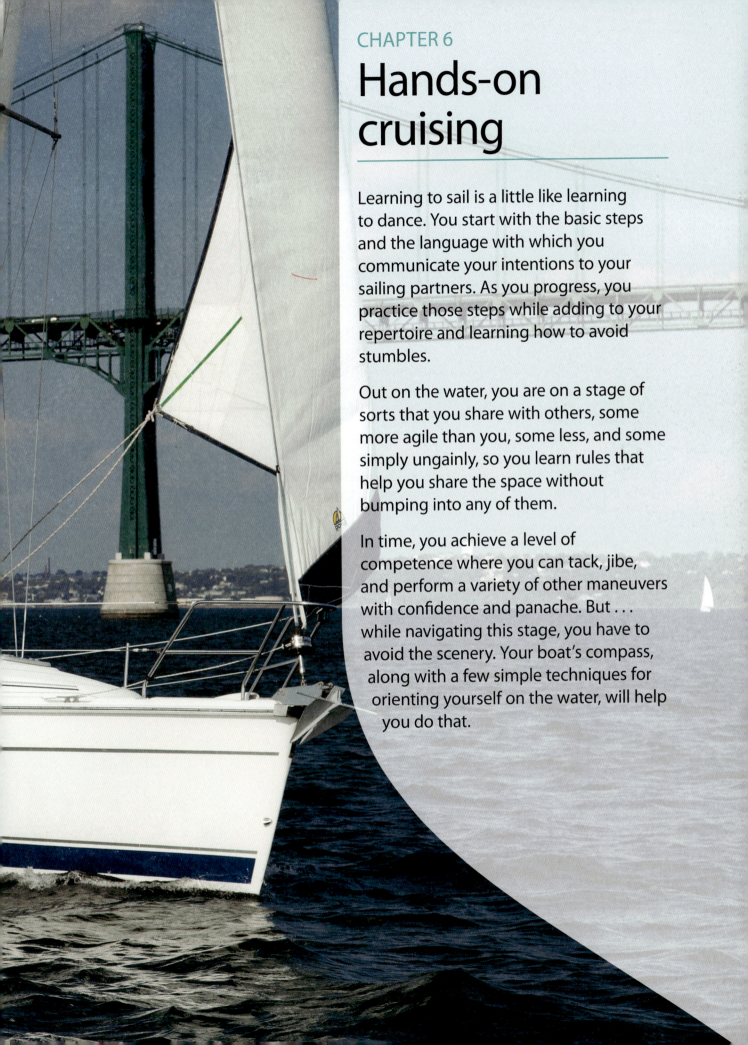

CHAPTER 6

Hands-on cruising

Learning to sail is a little like learning to dance. You start with the basic steps and the language with which you communicate your intentions to your sailing partners. As you progress, you practice those steps while adding to your repertoire and learning how to avoid stumbles.

Out on the water, you are on a stage of sorts that you share with others, some more agile than you, some less, and some simply ungainly, so you learn rules that help you share the space without bumping into any of them.

In time, you achieve a level of competence where you can tack, jibe, and perform a variety of other maneuvers with confidence and panache. But . . . while navigating this stage, you have to avoid the scenery. Your boat's compass, along with a few simple techniques for orienting yourself on the water, will help you do that.

THE COMPASS AT WORK

At sea, where the horizon is uniform and offers no reference point, steering a steady course is an art. With practice, you can steer by keeping the boat at a consistent angle to the wind or the waves, or use a slow-moving cloud as a "skymark." But to determine what direction to point the boat in the first place, you need the compass.

THE COMPASS AND STEERING

In Chapter 5, you saw how the compass works, how the numbers and letters on the compass card relate to the world around us, and how to plot a compass course on the chart. The next step is to steer a course using your boat's compass as a reference.

STEERING A COMPASS COURSE

We'll begin while motoring, so that course changes won't involve trimming the sails. Take the boat to an area of open water where you can perform some maneuvers without getting in the way of other boats. As you make your way there, watch how the compass card turns when you change direction.

Actually, the compass card does not turn. Its magnet ensures that the card maintains the same orientation relative to Earth's magnetic field. It appears to turn because the lubber's line, which is fixed to the body of the compass, and therefore to the boat, moves around the card as the boat changes direction.

STEERING EXERCISES

Pick a fixed point, a landmark or a navigation aid, and steer toward it. Look down at the compass and note the number on the compass card that's adjacent to the lubber's line.

Think of the lubber's line as the boat's bow. The point of the compass adjacent to the lubber's line — N, 30, 60, 90, etc. — is the direction the boat is pointing, its *heading*.

Turn the boat a little. As you do so, the lubber's line moves around the card as the boat's heading changes. Turn back so you are heading toward your mark again and note your heading.

As you steer a steady course, keeping the bow lined up with your mark, glance back and forth between the compass and your mark. That helps you relate the

movements of the lubber's line to those of the boat.

While someone keeps a lookout, have a crewmember stand in front of you so you can't see your mark.

Try to keep the boat on its heading. Make small movements with the steering wheel and watch the lubber's line as you turn a little to port, then a little to starboard, to see how much it moves around the compass card.

COMPASS TAG — A FUN DRILL

Ask a crewmember to give you a course to steer, say 045° (NE). After you've

steadied the boat on 045°, ask for another course. If the call was "210 degrees," you would look for 210° on the compass card, then think about which way to turn to bring you to that course the soonest. In this case you would turn to starboard. If you turned to port you'd have to turn the boat through 195 degrees to get there instead of through 165 degrees.

Make your turn gently and begin to correct the helm before you reach the new course.

Repeat the course-change exercise a few times while motoring to get a feel for it before trying it under sail. Remember to designate a lookout because the helmsman is going to be very focused on steering.

TIP *So you don't leave a snaky wake, use the top-dead-center mark on the wheel as a reference and keep your helm movements to the minimum.*

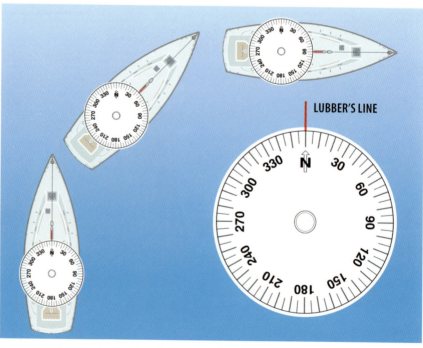

LUBBER'S LINE

The compass card maintains its orientation to Earth's magnetic field while the boat, and the lubber's line, rotate around it.

THE COMPASS AS A REFERENCE

Steering while staring at the compass is tiring and keeps your eyes inside the boat when you should be watching the sails and the water around you. It's usually easier to use an object ahead of the boat as a reference and confirm your heading by glancing periodically at the compass. However, there are times, such as when sailing in a current or in poor visibility, when you must pay closer attention to the compass to stay on course.

Currents affect the course you steer. Look for clues to their presence, like the wake trailing this buoy.

COURSE CHECK

Say you are setting off toward a destination but you are not sure, just by looking ahead, that you are going in the right direction. After all, one distant point of land is often indistinguishable from another. If you have plotted your course on the chart, you can use the compass to get the boat pointed in the right direction. Then, once you have a visual reference to refer to, you can steer by "eyeball." Remember, though, to check for the effects of currents and, if you are sailing, leeway.

CURRENT

Few bodies of water other than windless lakes are devoid of currents. Unless you sail in a tidal area and have studied the current tables (which ASA covers in ASA 105, Coastal Navigation), you may not be aware of the invisible force acting on your boat. Look for signs, such as buoys that are anchored but appear to be moving through the water.

COURSE CORRECTION

How can you tell if the boat is being affected by a current or leeway?

If you are steering toward a buoy, look at the land behind it.

Note the clump of trees, smokestack, house — whatever is directly in line with and behind the buoy. If your distant (rear) mark is sliding to the right of the buoy, the boat is being set to the right.

Turn the boat to port (left) to bring your marks back in line.

Steering the boat so your marks stay in line, note your heading (the number on the compass card next to the lubber's line). As long as you steer to that heading (and the current or your boat speed don't change), you will find the marks stay in line. Even though the bow is not pointing at your destination, the boat will maintain its course toward it and will not be carried toward any down-current hazard.

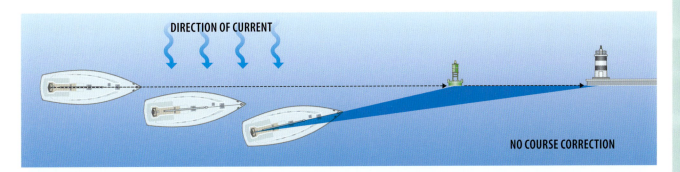

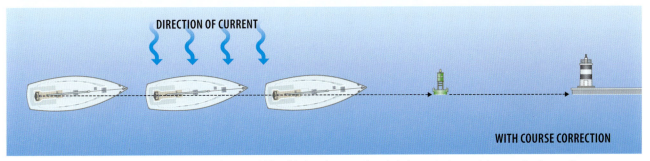

When steered at the buoy, top, the boat slides downstream. When steered "above" the buoy (up current from it), the boat maintains a straight course directly toward it.

SAILING A COMPASS COURSE

Maintaining a course is often easier under sail than when motoring. When you sail to the sails, changes in their trim, helm pressure, and the boat's angle of heel give you clues when you wander off course. Rather than keeping your gaze glued to the compass, you can watch the sails and the sea and glance at the compass from time to time to reassure yourself that you are on course.

THE COMPASS AND THE WIND

Sailors live by the wind, because the direction the wind is blowing determines where they can sail and at what speed. Without the compass, about all you can say about the wind direction is, "It's blowing from over there." Now, with the compass, you can give the wind's direction a name or a number.

You can say it's a northwest wind or a southerly wind, for example (a term like southerly indicates the wind is coming from that general direction). If you need

more precision, you can determine that the wind is from 315°, or 173°.

TIP *Remember, a wind's direction indicates where it is blowing* **from**. *A north wind is blowing from the north.*

If our wind today is a north wind, that has implications for the courses we wish to sail. Anywhere between northwest (315°) and northeast (045°) is in the no-sail zone. To get there, we'll have to

When sailing to windward, you can steer to the sails and use a landmark as a reference for your compass heading.

sail close-hauled and tack. You'll find that weather conditions and the point of sail affect how much you steer to the compass.

HEADERS AND LIFTS AND CLOSEST TACK

Let's assume you want to reach a destination that's due north (0°) and the wind is blowing from the north. You can't sail in the no-sail zone, approximately 45 degrees either side of north, so you have to beat to windward, sailing part of the way on port tack and part of the way on starboard tack. If you are on port tack (the wind blowing onto the port side of the boat) you will be sailing at about 045° until the wind changes.

The wind seldom blows steadily from one direction but fluctuates, shifting left and right. If you

are steering to the sails and the wind shifts left 15 degrees, you will see from the compass that you are now steering about 030°. This windshift is a *lift*; the wind has shifted away from your bow and you have been *lifted* to a course that brings you closer to your destination than your original course of 045°.

Your friends, sailing nearby on starboard tack at 315° before the shift, would now find themselves sailing at 300°. For them, the same shift was a *header* — the wind shifted forward, forcing them to *head down* to prevent the sails from luffing.

In a header, the wind shifts toward your bow; in a lift, away from your bow.

You got lucky with that wind shift because port tack is now the *closest tack* to your destination.

Your friends, seeing how you were lifted while they were headed, might tack over to port so they, too, are on the closest tack.

Whenever you are trying to reach a destination that's in the no-sail zone, you want to start out sailing on the closest tack. Use the compass to determine which tack that is.

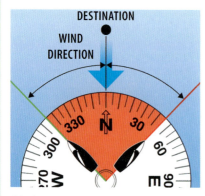  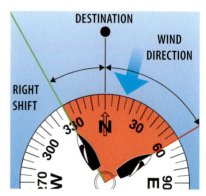

If the destination is north and the wind is north, port tack and starboard tack are equally favored. A wind shift to the left is a lift to the sailboat on port tack and a header to the boat on starboard tack, and puts the port-tack boat on the closest tack to the destination. A right shift is a header to the boat on port tack and a lift to the boat on starboard tack.

CLOSE-HAULED

When sailing close-hauled, you have no choice but to steer to the sails rather than to the compass. This is because the wind is never rock steady in strength or direction. To make the best speed, you adjust your heading and sometimes the sail trim to accomodate its fluctuations. Nevertheless, you always want to know in what direction you are going, and the compass tells you that. By glancing at it from time to time, you can estimate the average course you are making.

With the help of the compass, you can also identify wind shifts.

TACKING ANGLE

You know that your boat tacks through approximately 90 degrees (from one side of the no-sail zone to the other). Using the compass, you can estimate your heading for the next tack: If you are tacking from port tack to starboard tack, deduct 90 degrees from your port-tack heading; if tacking from starboard to port, add 90 degrees to your starboard-tack heading.

CLOSE REACH

When sailing on a close reach, your sheets are eased just a little and you again steer more to the sails than to the destination, especially if the wind is

shifty. If you're looking for speed, steer to the sail trim and keep track of your average compass heading. If course is more important (in poor visibility, for example, or when you have to stay clear of shoals), steer to the compass and have the crew adjust trim as necessary.

BEAM REACH TO BROAD REACH

On these points of sail, you will begin to notice how waves can affect the steering. Maintaining a steady compass course is quite difficult as the forces on the rudder (which you feel through the wheel or tiller) change significantly as the waves pass under the hull and the boat rolls. The compass card will appear to swing from side to side (it's really the boat rotating under it!) and your goal will be to average out either side of your course. Steering to a fixed mark is often easier in these conditions, but keep an eye on the

Since sailboats tack through about 90 degrees, the helmsman can use the compass to predict the next course.

compass to ensure you don't wander off course due to the challenging steering conditions and/or current.

RUNNING

When running dead downwind, your most important concern is to avoid an accidental jibe. You steer to the wind, especially if it's shifty, but the compass can be a big help in keeping you oriented if you have no fixed mark to steer toward.

LEEWAY

Although a sailboat is subject to leeway on all points of sail, its magnitude is greatest when sailing upwind or close reaching and the boat is well heeled.

Leeway has the same effect on your boat's actual course as a current running across it, except leeway always acts in the same direction relative to the boat — to leeward.

Check for leeway (or the combined effect of leeway and any current you might be sailing in) by using fixed references as described on page 103, and adjust your course to account for it.

ORIENTATION ON THE WATER

When trying to pinpoint your whereabouts in a strange city, you can look for street signs, big buildings emblazened with corporate names, and other recognizable landmarks that you can locate on the street map. You do the same when navigating in unfamiliar waters, except that you'll not see a big sign identifying the promontary that is Bloody Point. You have to use deduction, the chart, and the compass to figure out whether the point you are looking at is or is not Bloody Point.

NORTH UP

By convention, nautical charts are printed so that north is at the top of the sheet. An easy way to orient yourself relative to the chart is to stand next to the compass so you are facing north and turn the chart so that north on the chart aligns with north on the compass. Now you can study the land masses and other features around you and compare them to what you see on the chart.

GETTING YOUR BEARINGS

If you ever wondered where that expression comes from, you're about to find out. What follows is a simple exercise you can try while the boat is at the dock or, to make it more of a challenge, in open water (in which case your instructor

can help by indicating where your boat is located on the chart).

While marking your position on the chart, look at your surroundings. Pick a prominent feature that might be shown on the chart, such as a lighthouse or a chimney.

Now look across the center of the compass at that feature, let's say it's a chimney, and note the number on the compass card that roughly lines up with it — let's say it's 60 degrees.

On the chart, using the compass rose for reference, trace from your position in the general direction of 60 degrees and find your chimney.

What you are doing in this exercise is taking a rough *compass bearing* on the feature. In ASA 105, Coastal Navigation,

you will learn how to precisely plot the boat's position by taking accurate bearings. For now, you are getting a feel for the neighborhood (while your instructor keeps track of which exact street corner you are on).

You can reverse the exercise by picking a feature on the chart, establishing a bearing to it by referring to the compass rose on the chart, and looking over the boat's compass to find it in the real world.

RELATIVE POSITIONS

Without doing elaborate chartwork, you can gain a great deal of information about your position and your progress along your course by watching how the visual composition of the landscape and seascape changes as you sail along. Features nearer the boat "pass by" faster than features farther away — a beacon near the shoreline crosses your field of view quickly while a distant hilltop remains there for a long time. When under way, you can trace the boat's movement "across the chart" by watching how the bearings to features change.

If you have drawn your course on the chart, you can mark your progress by noting the times at which a sequence of landmarks or navigation marks come abeam. And if you measure the distance on the chart from one mark to the next, you can calculate your average speed.

Let's say you are heading southwest (225°). A landmark that was to your south (bearing 180°) will move slowly toward the east. At some point, its bearing will be 135° (southeast) — and it will be *abeam*. Later, it will be east of you (bearing 90°).

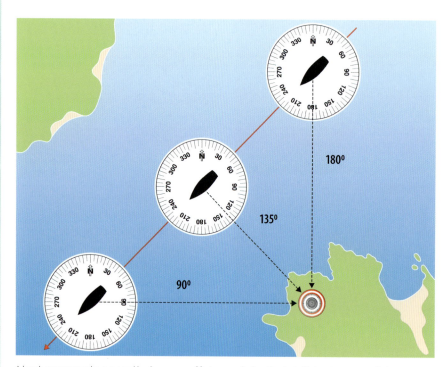

A boat's progress can be measured by the passage of features marked on the chart. Timing the passage of a known distance can give the boat's speed, and knowledge of the boat's speed allows distances to be calculated.

TRANSITS

There will be a moment when a closer feature and one farther away line up — one *transits* the other.

If you can identify both features on the chart, draw a line on the chart from the farther mark through the nearer mark and across the water. At the moment the transit occurred, you were somewhere along that line. If you have been steering accurately to your course, you are where the transit line crosses the course line you drew on the chart; if not, you are to one side or the other. Still, you have a pretty good idea of your position without doing any math.

You can use transits to establish when you have safely cleared a hazard, as the diagram on this page shows.

TIP *We use transits all the time in everyday life, though, most of the time, unconsciously. At what instant do you turn the steering wheel of your car to turn out of your driveway and into the street without running over the curb?*

RANGES

When you sail on the course that keeps the two marks in line, you are using them as a *range*. (Yes, you already used a range to check for current and leeway.)

In many places where ship channels zigzag between areas of shoal water, the government places ATONs to create ranges to guide vessels along each reach of the channel.

TIP *Sailing along a range is usually easier, and less prone to error, than sailing to a compass course. As you become familiar with your sailing area, you can create your own ranges to guide you as you enter your home port or your favorite anchorages.*

A range consists of a front mark and a higher back mark some distance behind it. Ranges are especially helpful in areas where currents may set across the

channel. When you sail along the range keeping the range marks in line, you are in the channel, even though your bow may be pointing to one side or the other to offset the current and/or leeway.

PREPARING FOR POOR VISIBILITY

An easy sail on a clear sunny day can suddenly become a challenge when rain or fog arrives to obscure your landmarks.

Before the gloom descends, use the techniques described above to establish your position as accurately as you can. Plot your route, toward home or a safe

haven, write down the headings and distances for each leg, and note the characteristics of any aids to navigation you can use to confirm your position.

Steer carefully to the compass and record the boat's speed so you can estimate the time (distance divided by speed) each leg will take to sail.

TIP *A watch with a countdown timer or a diver's bezel is handy when piloting in poor visibility. If you set the time when you should arrive at your next mark, you'll know when to start looking for it.*

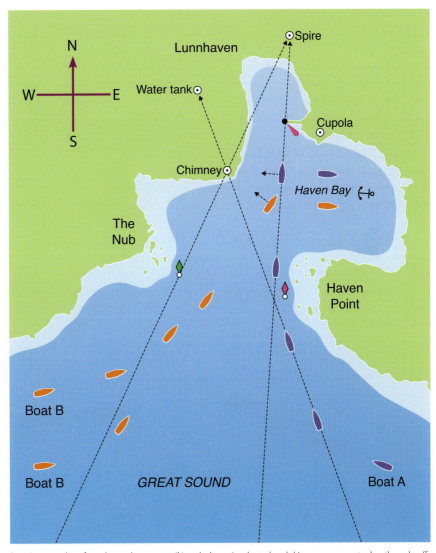

Boat A, approaching from the southeast, can sail into the bay using the tank and chimney as a range to clear the rocks off Haven Point, then use the end of the jetty and the spire to its north as a new range. Boats B, approaching from the west, can turn and head for the cupola once the spire has transited to the right of the chimney. Both boats can turn safely into the anchorage in Haven Bay when the chimney is abeam. The ranges will likely be visible before the buoys.

ANCHORING

Cruising isn't all sailing. One of the great gifts of sailing is that it provides a way to get to places far and near that may only be accessible by water. By anchoring, you can stay there — for a week, a night, or for lunch — to enjoy the scenery and pursue favorite activities like swimming, beachcombing, hiking, or reading.

ANCHORING LORE

Many cruising sailors spend more time at anchor than doing anything else: more time than sailing and certainly, if they are on a budget or prefer solitude, more time than tied up in a marina. Anchoring is therefore an important subject in a sailor's book of knowledge and a popular topic of conversation anywhere cruisers gather. While all sailors have their favorite anchors and methods of setting them, most agree on the fundamentals.

ANCHOR TYPES

A primitive anchor depends on weight for its *holding power*, its ability to resist being pulled across the seabed by the boat to which it's attached. That suffices on a small craft, but on a bigger boat with greater windage (the area of the hull, superstructure, and rig exposed to the wind), such an anchor becomes too heavy to handle. Anchors have evolved, and sailors today can choose from a wide variety of designs that rely less on weight than on their ability to dig into the seabed and resist being pulled through it.

Just how well an anchor can hold depends on its design and on the nature of the bottom. An anchor that holds well in soft sand may not do as well in mud or rocks. Cruising sailors who expect to anchor in a variety of bottoms carry

several anchors of different types. Sailors who stay local usually have a primary anchor that works reliably in their waters plus a backup. Bottom line, anchors all have to do the same thing, which is to attach your boat securely to the seabed and not budge.

GROUND TACKLE

The anchor together with its rode, which might be rope, chain, or a combination of both, is called *ground tackle*, and you might need different ground tackle for different anchoring situations.

Chain is heavy, which helps the anchor to hold, and its weight acts as a shock absorber in gusty winds. However, its weight makes chain difficult to raise and lower by hand, and usually requires that a windlass be installed to handle it.

A typical cruising boat carries an anchor on its bow and has a windlass and storage locker for the rode.

Rope is much lighter and easier to handle than chain but can chafe through if used around rocks. A rope rode is almost always connected to its anchor by a length of chain, which also adds holding power.

Rope absorbs shock loads by stretching. Nylon is the favored fiber for rope anchor rodes because of its ability to stretch.

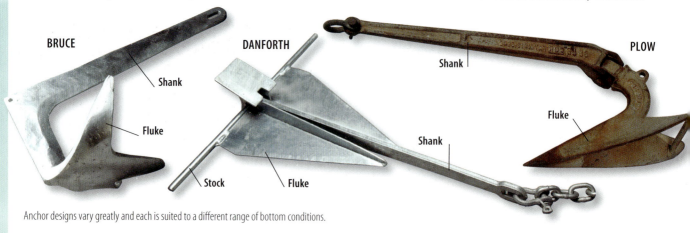

BRUCE   Shank   Fluke

DANFORTH   Stock   Fluke

PLOW   Shank   Shank   Fluke

Anchor designs vary greatly and each is suited to a different range of bottom conditions.

THE ANCHORAGE

Where you anchor is all-important. The perfect anchorage will have enough depth at low tide but not too much at high tide, lots of swinging room, a bottom with good holding, shelter from wind and seas, and no mosquitoes.

CHARTED INFORMATION

All of that information (except the mosquito part) you can obtain from the chart. Check the wind direction (and the weather forecast) to see which coves or bays might be suitable in present and expected conditions (and look for alternatives in case the forecast proves wrong). As you saw in Chapter 5, the chart will tell you the depths and also the nature of the bottom. For reliable holding, look for sand (S), mud (M) or clay (Cl) bottoms. Try to avoid rocks (Rk) because anchors can become trapped.

Do not anchor in marked channels or anywhere that is marked on the chart as prohibited, such as restricted areas and cable crossings. In busy harbors there may be designated anchorages for pleasure craft that you must use.

SCOPE

An anchor's ability to hold depends to a great degree on the angle at which the rode is pulling on it. Most anchors will withstand a pull from horizontal to a few degrees above horizontal and *trip* (pull out) when the pull is vertical.

The angle at which the rode pulls on the anchor is determined by the *scope*, the ratio of the length of rode used to the distance from the boat's bow to the seabed.

A common practice is to use 7:1 scope

This anchored boat is complying with the Navigation Rules by displaying the black ball.

for rope-and-chain rode. To calculate how much rode to deploy, add the height of the boat's bow above the water to the depth where the anchor will lie and multiply the total by 7.

Because of its weight, chain hangs in a curve between the bow and the anchor, so the angle at which it pulls on the anchor is very small — until the chain becomes taut. Much of the time the weight of the chain alone is holding the boat. In normal situations, this means a scope of 5:1 is adequate with an all-chain rode.

If you let out only enough rode for the anchor to reach the bottom, it will pull upward on the anchor as soon as the boat moves. That, obviously, won't be secure.

TIP *Estimate the scope you need from the depth marked on the chart in the place you decide to anchor. Remember that this depth is for low tide. To figure for high tide, you will need the tide tables for that area.*

TIP *Most areas where people cruise, under sail or power, are described in detail in cruising guides for which someone has already done the hard work of evaluating anchorages (including the mosquito factor). Use these books (as guides, not gospel) to help you choose your anchorages.*

For a rope-and-chain rode, scope is ideally 7:1 — the length of rode deployed is 7x the depth at the anchor plus freeboard at the boat's bow. With too little scope, the anchor will simply pull out of the bottom.

h (height)
d (depth)

INADEQUATE SCOPE

SCOPE
(d+h) x 7

ADEQUATE SCOPE

WIND DIRECTION

A chain rode will lie on the bottom until the wind pressure on the boat is sufficient to lift it, when its weight acts like a spring to absorb shock loads.

CHAIN RODE IN WIND   **CHAIN RODE IN CALM**

CHOOSING THE SPOT TO ANCHOR

As you approach your chosen anchorage, look around to check its salient features so that you can place yourself visually (remember those transits?). If boats are already anchored there, motor slowly around the anchorage and observe how they are lying and see where you might find a spot with adequate swinging room.

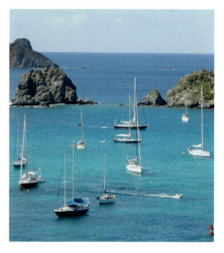

Popular anchorages often fill up early, and latecomers must respect the rights of boats already anchored by not anchoring too close to them.

SWINGING ROOM

A boat at anchor usually lies downwind of the anchor with the bow pointing toward the anchor. If the wind direction changes, the boat will change position (as will the other boats in the anchorage). That means you need *swinging room*, a circle around the anchor clear of obstructions, including other boats, in which to swing. The radius of that circle is the length of the boat plus the length of rode let out plus some safety room.

RESPECT YOUR NEIGHBORS

Note how the boats are anchored — to one anchor, to two anchors off the bow, or to an anchor at bow and stern — as that will affect how they swing. In tidal areas, boats might swing to the tide.

It's an unwritten rule that boats already at anchor have right of occupation over later arrivals. If you anchor too close to another boat and a wind change brings you together, as last one in, you must *weigh anchor* (raise it up) and leave.

PREPARING THE ANCHOR

You know from the chart the depth of the water at low tide. Add to that the tidal range (see page 133) to obtain the depth of the water at high tide and use that to calculate how much rode you will need for your desired scope.

If you have a rope rode with a short length of chain, you can fake out the chain and line on the deck.

....

TIP *Most rodes are marked at intervals so you can tell how much you are letting out. If yours is not, fake it out in measured lengths, say of 5 feet.*

....

Make the rode fast to a cleat at the point where you will have your desired scope set. Make sure the bitter end of the rode, too, is made fast.

A boat with an all-chain rode should have a windlass, with which you control the chain as you pay it out. The chain will be in a chain locker belowdecks with its

bitter end, you hope, lashed to a fixture up high in the locker where you can reach it with a knife in an emergency. The chain should also be marked with painted links at measured intervals so you will know how much you have paid out.

Ready the anchor itself by undoing any lashings or removing any pins that secure it in its stowage. Free it so it is ready to be lowered when the moment arrives.

....

TIP *Anchors are stowed in many ways and in different places from boat to boat. Your instructor will provide explicit directions for readying the anchor on the teaching boat.*

....

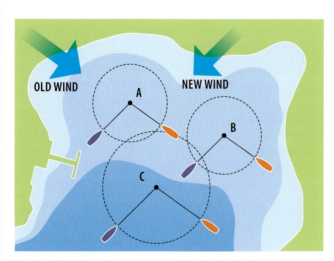

Boats A and B had plenty of swinging room until Boat C anchored in deeper water on longer scope. All is well if the wind holds steady, but a calm might bring a conflict.

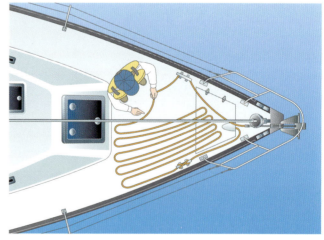

Faking out a rope rode ensures it will pay out without snagging. It's made fast at the desired scope and the crew can control it as it pays out by snubbing it on a cleat.

COPING WITH WEATHER

As carefully as we lay our plans, the weather often manages to inject a little uncertainty and the occasional surprise. Handling a gradual increase in wind strength is one thing: Reef early and think about seeking shelter. A sudden squall requires quick and decisive action. Always be on the alert for changes in the weather and have plans ready so you can take appropriate action.

TIP *Whenever you are on the water, watch the sky for signs of the wind's behavior. A change in clouds can signal a change in wind direction. A darkening of the water's surface indicates more wind ; if whitecaps appear, too, a **lot** more wind. Look at other sailboats — what points of sail they are on and how they are heeling.*

SUMMER THUNDERSTORM

Hot humid air rising off the land is the engine behind a weather event that pops up in many sailing regions: the summer-afternoon thunderstorm.

You see the early signs in the form of puffy *cumulus* clouds. As the day wears on, some grow into rather bigger clouds with tall cauliflower tops.

Those cauliflowers are *cumulonimbus*, which very often become thunderstorms and signal their intensity with the characteristic anvil-shaped top. Even a hint of such a cloud on a hot and humid day will have an experienced skipper looking for an escape route.

Driven by upper-level winds, these storms often approach against the sea breeze and, as well as lightning, can pack winds of 40 knots or more, mostly at the leading edge. Depending on how far away you spot the cloud, you might have from 30 minutes to two hours to take shelter or batten down the hatches.

Shelter would be your home port or a cove that's protected on the side from which the storm is approaching and where you have time to drop the anchor and set it hard.

With enough of a head start, you might be able to minimize your exposure to the storm by steering away from it on a course at 90 degrees to its path.

If it appears you'll be caught in it, make preparations:

■ Turn on the VHF radio and tune it to the Wx channel (or check your smart-phone or computer weather app) to learn about the storm's intensity and path.

■ Head toward an area where you have open navigable water to leeward.

When you see the rainbow, it usually means the summer afternoon thunder squall has passed by. If this were morning, you'd be looking west and the cloud, with heavy rain and probably very strong (if short lived) wind, is headed toward you.

■ Insist everybody wear a life jacket.
■ Have anyone who might be sent out of the cockpit put on a safety harness.
■ Close all ports and hatches.
■ Make sure the anchor is ready to be deployed.
■ Start the engine.
■ Drop and furl the sails and secure them well.
■ Scan the sea around the boat and note the locations of any other vessels (and their courses), aids to navigation, or potential hazards.
■ Put on your waterproof clothing.
■ If there's lightning, send most of the crew below and instruct everyone to stay away from metal, such as the rigging.
■ Switch the VHF to Channel 16 (see page 134).
■ Wait for it . . . .

When the storm hits, all will be pandemonium for a few minutes — a wall of stinging rain, flashes of lightning, and a howling wind. No problem: The sails are down so they won't get damaged and the boat is under control.

If you have sea room to leeward, you can let the boat take care of itself and blow downwind.

If you don't have much sea room, or you think the storm might last awhile, use the engine to drive the boat slowly into the wind.

Usually, afternoon pop-up storms don't last long and the wind drops once the leading edge has passed over, but leave the sails down until you're sure it has blown over. Once the storm has passed, resume sailing or seek shelter, according to what the weather is offering up next.

FOG AND ITS KIN

Fog is no friend of the mariner, unless that mariner is a smuggler and thankful for the cover. For millennia, eyesight was the preeminent tool for establishing a position on the water, maintaining a course, and avoiding obstacles. Today we have GPS and radar, but neither one alleviates the feeling of vulnerability brought on by being surrounded by impenetrable fog.

FOG'S ORIGIN

Fog has several causes but the same factors are at work in all of them.

Air normally contains a quantity of water vapor, and the amount it can hold varies with temperature. Warm air can hold more moisture than cold air, but if that warm air cools down, it can reach a temperature,

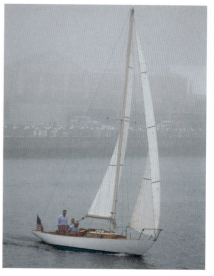

Coastal fog often occurs in seasons when the tempertatures of the water and the air are very different.

called the dew point, where it becomes saturated. Any further drop in temperature causes water to condense out of the air. At high elevations, we call this condensed water clouds. When it forms on or near the earth's surface, we call it fog.

Several mechanisms lead to the formation of fog but the one that most often operates in coastal waters is warm humid air moving over cool water. This occurs in spring and summer when the land heats up before the sea (it also happens around large lakes), and warms the air above it. If that warm air moves over the water and, cooled from beneath, reaches its dew point, fog will form over the surface of the water.

A similar mechanism is at work when the warm air mass behind a warm front moves over cooler water.

Fog is hard to predict and can be very localized. Land-centric weather forecasts, such as those put forth by TV stations, don't usually mention the possibility of sea fog forming, and even NOAA sometimes misses it in its marine forecasts.

As a general rule, if it's hot and humid ashore and the water is cold, be on the lookout for fog. If you can measure the air temperature and dewpoint (see below), you can gain insight into the conditions that create fog in your area.

ONBOARD WEATHER STATION

Meteorology, the science of weather, is a good hobby for a sailor (sailing isn't a hobby, it's a lifestyle!).

Meteorologists use a standard set of weather observations to establish the current synopsis (what is going on right now) and forecast what might occur in

the future locally and elsewhere. Those standard observations are:

- Barometric pressure (and tendency upward or downward)
- Temperature
- Humidity
- Dew point
- Wind speed
- Wind direction
- Cloud cover and type of clouds
- Precipitation

You can use the compass to figure wind direction and, with practice, observation to judge wind speed, but many cruising sailboats are equipped with wind instruments, which make life much easier. Inexpensive handheld instruments can provide data, such as temperature and dewpoint, so you can connect more of the weather dots. By matching yor own observations with forecasts and weather reports, you will learn how to read the weather signs in your sailing area.

Handheld weather instruments provide a range of data.

THE SHIP'S BAROMETER

After the eyes, the barometer is your most useful forecasting tool and it doesn't need batteries or an Internet connection.

A barometer tells you what the barometric pressure is currently, but more important, if you record the barometer readings in the log at regular intervals, you can identify trends in barometric pressure.

Rapid changes mean trouble ahead.

A steady barometer usually means that if the weather is to change, it will do so slowly. A falling barometer indicates a departing high pressure or an approaching low pressure. A rising barometer means the low has passed. Generally speaking, when the barometer is falling, be prepared for wind and rain from a low-pressure system — the faster it falls, the more wind. When the barometer is rising, expect the weather to brighten as the high pressure moves in. By the same token, if the barometer rises quickly, expect strong winds.

TIDES

Tides are the vertical movement of the water's surface — high tide occurs when it's at its highest level and low tide at its lowest. They are the result of the gravitational influence of the moon and the sun on the earth's seas and oceans.

EVER-CHANGING TIDES

The moon's influence dominates the tidal cycle, and the tides essentially follow it around the earth. Since the lunar month is 29 1/2 days, the tidal cycle occurs about 50 minutes later every day. And because of some rather complicated physics, the daily tidal cycle consists of two high tides about 12 hours apart and a low tide about six hours after each high tide.

Due to the sun's influence, the heights of high and low tides vary with the phase of the moon. At new moon, when the moon and sun are aligned on the same side of the earth, and at full moon, when they are aligned on opposite sides, their effects aggregate to create higher high tides and lower low tides, called *spring tides*. At the moon's first and last quarters, the sun's influence partly negates that of the moon to cause *neap tides*, when the tidal *range*, (the difference in height between high and low tide) is less.

TIDAL CURRENTS

Tidal currents are the result of of water moving horizontally between high tide and low tide. Their strength is affected by local factors such as the tidal range (which varies greatly from place to place) and the topography through which the water has to flow. Currents are stronger at spring tides than at neap tides.

Taking the simple example of a bay open to the ocean, as the tide comes in, from low tide to high tide, the current is a *flood* current. When the tide is going out, it's an *ebb* current. *Slack water* occurs when the current is neither flooding nor ebbing. The tidal current is strongest about midway between the periods of slack water, which are usually about six hours apart.

Geographical features affect tidal flow, and in many places slack water does not coincide with the times of high or low tide. You cannot assume that the current

will change at high tide and low tide.

In many coastal regions, the tidal range and the strength of tidal currents can affect your timing when planning a voyage and, when you are under way, your course to steer.

When sailing in a current, if you know its *set* (the direction it's flowing) and *drift* (its speed) you can adjust your course to account for it. The calculations for this are taught in ASA 105, Coastal Navigation. For your present purposes you can estimate a course correction from observations.

You can see the effect of a current on anchored buoys and fishing floats. A current flowing past a buoy creates a wake, just as if the buoy were moving through the water. You can estimate both the speed and the direction of the current by observing this wake. When sailing, you can use ranges to see if you are being set by a current, as described in Chapter 5.

TIDE AND CURRENT TABLES

In the US, tidal predictions are generated by NOAA. All the information you'll ever need is available at NOAA on the Web (www.tidesandcurrents.noaa.gov) including tide tables and current tables for many locations on the Atlantic, Gulf, and Pacific coasts.

NOAA also publishes tide tables and tidal current tables in book form, and these can be purchased through a variety of marine outlets. For local information in a reasonably compact form, look for regional publications that contain tide tables and current charts.

In some coastal regions, like Maine, those who make their living from the sea are governed by the tides. Low tide might not be the easiest time to leave the harbor, but it provides an opportunity to paint the boat's bottom or make repairs..

Both the strength and direction of a current can be estimated by observing its effect on buoys.

ELECTRONIC COMMUNICATIONS

Radio heralded a quantum leap in maritime communications and safety. Before radio, ships could only exchange messages if they were in sight of one another, which meant a ship's "horizon of rescue" was literally its visible horizon. Radio extended that horizon to any radio station — on a ship or on shore — within range. Today, satellites provide radio surveillance over most of the planet, and satellite phones allow sailors (and non-sailors) to call home from almost anywhere.

RADIOS, CELL PHONES, AND THE COASTAL SAILOR

For the coastal cruising sailor, the VHF radio is the lifeline of first resort. It is also an important tool for communicating safety-related information with other vessels and with the shore. Cell phones are of primary value in general communications and their use can enhance safety by taking non-urgent traffic off the radio frequencies.

BROADCAST SIGNALS

When you make a telephone call, only the party you call can hear you. A radio broadcasts a signal that any radio within range that is switched on and tuned to the same frequency will receive.

This makes VHF radio the best way to call for help on the water. While the Coast Guard, or some other authority, will likely hear your transmission, another vessel nearer your location might also hear it and be able to render assistance sooner. Also, the USCG VHF network is equipped to locate the source of a transmission, aiding in the effectiveness of a response.

With broadcast transmissions, however, if everybody tries to talk at the same time, nobody can talk. Radio communications require users to adhere to an established etiquette — and it's backed up by regulations.

RADIO STATIONS

Any boat or shore facility with a radio transmitter is, in radio lingo, a station. With some exceptions, a radio station must be licensed by the Federal Communications Commission (FCC).

Pleasure craft under 65 feet operating within US waters are exempted from the requirement to obtain a station license.

Commercial vessels are required by federal regulations to carry a VHF transmitter, for which they must obtain a station license.

DIGITAL SELECTIVE CALLING

All new VHF radios have Digital Selective Calling (DSC). At the press of a button, a DSC-equipped set will send an automated distress call that will trigger a response from the USCG Rescue 21 system.

When the set is properly installed, registered, assigned a Maritime Mobile Service Identity (MMSI) number, and connected to a GPS receiver, the automated call includes information on the vessel sending it, including its position.

DSC also enables you to use the VHF radio much as you do a telephone — it effectively "dials" the MMSI number of the vessel you wish to call, eliminating the open-airwave hail.

CHANNEL 16

A marine VHF radio can broadcast and receive on about three dozen channels, each of which has a designated use.

Channel 16 has special significance as the "International Distress, Safety, and Calling" channel on which calls between stations (one of which must be a vessel) are initiated. Once contact is made, both stations must switch to a *working channel* to conduct their conversation. The USCG monitors Channel 16 24/7.

A vessel that is required to carry a radio must monitor Channel 16 at all times when the vessel is in operation. The ASA recommends pleasure craft carry a VHF radio and monitor Channel 16 when on the water.

NOTE To reduce non-urgent traffic on Channel 16, the FCC has designated Channel 9 as a calling channel for recreational boats for non-urgent communications. Many marine VHF radios can maintain a watch on two and even three channels, so you can monitor channels 9 and 16 simultaneously.

WORKING CHANNELS

Under FCC regulations, each marine VHF channel has a designated use.

Channel 13 is for "bridge-to-bridge" communications, that is, between ships' bridges, for navigational safety purposes. (It is also used to communicate with operators of bridges that span navigable waterways and must be opened to allow marine traffic to pass.)

Channels 68, 69, and 71 are working channels for ship-to-ship and ship-to-coast communications. Channel 72 is for ship-to-ship use only.

NOTE Ship-to-ship is radio jargon, and size is irrelevant. If you call the USS *Enterprise* from your daysailer, that's ship-to-ship. Calling the marina from your boat is ship-to-shore.

USING A VHF RADIO

When you turn on a marine radio, it tunes to Channel 16. To change channels, you scroll up or down, much like on a car radio. It has a volume control and a squelch control with which to "shut out" background radio noise.

To transmit, press and hold the button on the microphone. Squeeze this button only while you are talking and release it to listen. Because the radio transmits and receives on the same frequency (simplex), you must release the transmit button to open up the frequency and to be able to hear a response.

The transmitter has two power settings. Use low power when calling stations within sight (and always when using Channel 13) and high power for calls over greater distances.

VHF transmissions operate over "line of sight," and their range is limited by the earth's curvature. The higher the antenna, the greater the potential range.

STANDARD CALL PROTOCOL

For non-urgent calls, listen to the channel for 15 seconds or so to make sure you won't be treading on anyone else's transmission. Use Channel 16 (in most areas of the US) to call other boats and Channel 13 to call a ship or bridge for navigational purposes. Select the high- or low-power setting as appropriate.

If you are aboard *Joshua* and wish to contact your buddies aboard *Spray*, use the succinct format that follows. It keeps the transmission short, freeing up air time for other users.

"*Spray, Spray, Spray*, this is *Joshua*."
"*Joshua*, this is *Spray*, over."
"*Spray*, switch to channel six eight, over."
"Switching to six eight."

After *Spray* acknowledges your call, switch to Channel 68 and listen again for other conversations. If the channel is clear, call *Spray* again:

"*Spray, Spray, Spray*, this is *Joshua*."
"*Joshua*, this is *Spray*, over."

Keep the conversation brief and use "over" when you stop talking to tell *Spray* that you are listening for a response.

When finished, you say, "*Joshua* out," and switch back to Channel 16.

In other situations, identify your vessel as "the yacht *Joshua*."

TIP *You can use the VHF only for legitimate ship's business. It's OK to arrange a rendezvous with Spray in Indian River but chatting about the Redskins game could incur a penalty.*

URGENT RADIO TRANSMISSIONS

All radio stations must heed high-priority calls, which fall into three distinct categories. "Mayday" declares that an imminent threat exists of the loss of your vessel or of life aboard it. "Pan Pan" prefaces an urgent transmission regarding the safety of a vessel or person when there is no imminent threat of loss of life or of the vessel. "Securité," announces a message containing urgent safety information regarding a hazard to navigation.

MAYDAY

You begin a Mayday with the distress call, which is very brief:

"Mayday, Mayday, Mayday,
This is the yacht *Joshua, Joshua, Joshua*."

Follow up immediately with the distress message, in which you provide details of your vessel, position, the nature of your distress, and the assistance you require:

"Mayday, This is the yacht *Joshua*."

"I am in position . . . (give latitude and longitude or position relative to an ATON or geographic feature).

"I am taking on water . . . (give the nature of your distress).

"I need . . . (describe assistance needed — medical, evacuation, etc.).

"My vessel is a 30-foot white sailboat . . . (describe your vessel).

"There are four persons aboard . . . (provide number of people aboard).

The responding Coast Guard operator will take control of the situation and elicit more information as needed.

PAN PAN

Pan Pan (pronounced pahn pahn) is delivered in the same way as a Mayday but with "Pan Pan" repeated three times at the beginning, normally followed by, "all stations," the name of the station calling, and the message.

The Coast Guard will use Pan Pan to advise "all ships" to be on the lookout for a vessel in trouble or missing.

You would use Pan Pan if you need assistance (lost steering for example) but are not in imminent danger, or if you saw another boat in distress.

SECURITÉ

Use Securité (pronounced se-cu-ri-tay) to report a hazard to navigation, such as dangerous floating debris or a missing or damaged aid to navigation. A Securité call requires no response.

NOTE Radio operators who monitor a dozen radios simultaneously at rescue centers say that "Mayday" always gets their attention. However, do not use Mayday in a non-life-threatening situation lest you divert attention from a genuinely life-threatening incident elsewhere. Perpetrators of hoax Mayday calls are subject to severe penalties.

A VHF radio is useful for making (and hearing) urgent calls but a cell phone is better for conversations.

HANDLING EMERGENCIES

By taking this ASA course, you are on a path toward acquiring the skills and knowledge you need to make sound decisions when sailing and to ensure the boat's equipment is in good condition. Still, stuff happens, and a good way to further build self reliance is to examine the kinds of mishaps that can occur on a sailboat and put plans in place for dealing with them.

MISHAP OR EMERGENCY?

The difference between comedy and tragedy is often a matter of degree. A poor soul who slips while stepping from dock to boat might simply be the object of guffaws if all he suffers is a loss of dryness and dignity and a nearby ladder offers an easy exit. If he were to hit his head on the way down, or if there were no ladder or anyone to witness his fall, the outcome could be much more dire.

If your onboard "situation" becomes an emergency, one way to signal other boats is with a smoke flare.

CONTINGENCY PLANS

You can take precautions, but you should also have remedies available to help you recover from mishaps so they don't become emergencies if they do occur. In the following pages, we'll examine some possible incidents and propose ways of mitigating their effects.

SHORESIDE CONTACTS

Before leaving the dock, make sure you have the phone numbers of important contacts in your cell phone. These would include a designated person ashore whom you would call in case you change

your plans, the marina, a commercial towing service, and the local USCG station. In the event of a breakdown, you then have instant access to assistance.

CALLING FOR ASSISTANCE

In an emergency that threatens or has caused injury, your first resort is VHF 16. Everyone with "ears on" will hear you.

Your second line is a direct call to the USCG by cell phone.

A 911 call is potentially the least effective, as the 911 dispatcher will in turn have to call the Coast Guard to relay your information.

If you have suffered a breakdown but are not in imminent danger, call the tow service or the marina, not the Coast Guard. **NOTE** There was a time when the Coast Guard would respond to almost all calls for assistance. Now, unless there has been an injury or an immediate threat to life exists, it will direct you to call a professional towing company.

....

TIP *Experience will teach you how to determine whether an incident is an irritant you can remedy with onboard resources or an emergency. If there's any doubt, call for help.*

....

TOWING AND BEING TOWED

Boaters of all kinds sometimes find themselves in need of a tow. A powerboat might suffer engine failure or a sailboat could have a rigging snarl-up and a line around the propeller.

Towing is hazardous and in any but the calmest conditions is best left to professionals who have the proper equipment and the training to use it.

Because of the high loads involved, a towline must be tied to very strong points on both boats. On a sailboat, the strongest points are the base of the mast

or the primary winches.

Towing is best done with a *bridle*, two lines made up in a Y. The upper points of the Y are two ends of one line. When towing with a sailboat, these should be made fast on the primary winches. Tie the leg of the Y to the center of this line and attach it to the boat being towed, perhaps with another bridle led through the bow chocks.

Wherever possible, avoid pulling a sailboat stern first, because that can cause serious damage to the rudder.

Any time you are on a boat towing or being towed, stay well clear of the towline and its attachment points.

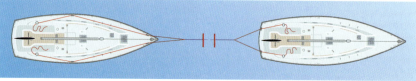
When towing, a bridle ensures the pull is centered and the load is evenly distributed.

RUNNING AGROUND

All sailors run aground at some time or another. It can be the result of inattention, carelessness, or the natural migration of a sandbar. A hard grounding on rock or coral can result in damage to the boat or injury to crew if the boat was sailing fast. A soft grounding in mud might only be embarrassing.

If the keel is simply resting on the bottom, heeling the boat might lift it enough to free it.

FIRST RESPONSE

Immediately stop the boat from sailing further into trouble by easing the sheets or by putting the engine in neutral. Take stock of the situation.

■ If it was a hard grounding, check the crew for injuries, then check for hull damage and leaks, especially around the rudder and keel.

■ Insist everyone put on a life jacket.

■ If you are on a lee shore, drop the sails so they don't drive you farther toward it.

■ If anyone is seriously injured or the boat has sustained major damage, call the Coast Guard.

■ Establish from the tide tables whether the tide is rising or falling.

GETTING OFF THE GROUND

Depending on the location, the nature of the bottom, and the design of the boat, several techniques are available for you to try singly or in combination to refloat the boat.

First, use the chart to figure out where you are and what direction you must move the boat to reach deeper water.

TIP *Before you ran aground, you were in deep enough water, so you know that you will refloat if you can get back there.*

If you were sailing slowly and hit gently, you may be able to back off with the engine. Make sure the rudder is free by gently turning the wheel to one side and then the other. If it is, ease the engine into reverse and see if that does the trick. As long as the rudder is not aground, you can try upping the rpm little by little.

Try heeling the boat to rotate the keel up off the bottom — so the boat draws less water — by moving all the crew to the leeward side. (This doesn't work with a wing keel!) To heel the boat more, you could have crew climb on the boom, then ease the sheet.

If you're still stuck, you have to do a few things quite quickly.

If the tide is rising, you're in luck. Drop the anchor (or set an anchor as a *kedge*) to hold you in place and wait until you float off.

If the deeper water is to leeward or ahead, use a combination of the sails and crew weight to heel the boat so the wind will blow you off.

If you are unable to free the boat, call for help from a professional towing company. Make this decision promptly, as it takes time for a towboat to respond and the tide waits for no man.

TIP *When sailing in waters of doubtful depth, favor the windward side of the channel so, if you do touch, you can sail off more easily.*

KEDGING OFF

Kedging is a time-honored technique used to work a boat to windward in confined waters or up a river. Today, it is most often used to free a grounded boat. To be able to *kedge off*, you have to transport a *kedge anchor* to deeper water. Every cruising sailboat should have aboard an anchor light enough it can be carried in a dinghy and a rope rode.

Make the bitter end of the rode fast on board the sailboat. Lower the anchor into the dinghy and slowly drive the dinghy to deeper water, paying out the rode as you go. When the rode is fully extended, ease the anchor off the dinghy (taking care to keep the rode clear of the outboard motor).

Haul on the rode to set the anchor, then apply steady tension while heeling the boat with crew weight.

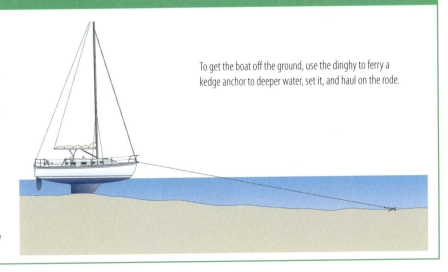

To get the boat off the ground, use the dinghy to ferry a kedge anchor to deeper water, set it, and haul on the rode.

RESPONDING TO A LEAK

Leaks run the gamut from the irritating to the catastrophic. Fortunately, the vast majority are in the first category and, other than causing a little discomfort and inconvenience, shouldn't put a damper on your sailing. However, if water is coming into the boat in significant quantities you must deal with it and its source as quickly as possible.

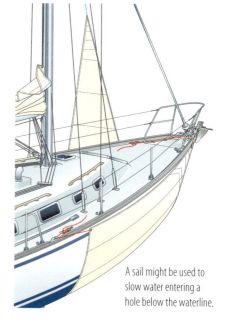

A sail might be used to slow water entering a hole below the waterline.

CLUES THAT YOU HAVE A LEAK

You know water is getting into the boat if:
- The automatic bilge pump goes on more than once every few hours or it runs continuously.
- Water is visible in the cabin welling up from under the cabin sole.
- Water comes out from under a sink cabinet or the head door.
- You lift a floorboard and there it is.

FINDING THE LEAK

While considering potential sources, determine how quickly water is entering. If it's fast, you must work quickly to find the cause.

Ensure the automatic bilge pump is activated and designate someone to operate the hand bilge pump.

Unless the boat has struck an object in the water, the prime suspects are holes that already exist in the hull.
- Through-hull fittings
Trace all the through-hull fittings (drains, water intakes, etc.) and close all the seacocks. There might be a diagram of their locations somewhere handy — in the chart table possibly.

TIP Don't shut off the engine raw-water seacock if the engine is running. However, if that is the source of your leak, first shut down the engine, then close the seacock.

In the unlikely event a seacock has failed, there should be a softwood plug tied to it that you can hammer into the opening.
- Propeller shaft and rudder stock
Where the propeller shaft and rudder stock penetrate the hull are potential locations for leaks. They are often difficult to reach, but you usually only have serious problems with them subsequent to an obvious incident — a hard grounding with the rudder, striking a floating object, or a line around the propeller — that would prompt you to look at those locations first.

STEMMING THE LEAK

Whatever the leak or its cause, you must improvise ways to stem it, for example by stuffing rags in it and bracing them in place with floorboards or other available material. If the hull has been holed, try to stanch it from the outside by tying lines

to a sail or mattress and manevering it over the opening.

Anyone who's not looking for the leak or working to stem it should be operating the pumps, electric and manual, and perhaps bailing with a bucket and dumping the water into the cockpit (from where it will drain overboard).

If the situation is manageable, head for the nearest location where you can deal with the problem, such as a marina with a haul-out facility.

DESPERATE MEASURES

If it proves impossible to stop the leak, pump and bail with all available means and assess the situation. If the boat (and therefore life) is threatened, call for help.

If you are able to sail or motor the boat, try to take it to a sheltered area with shallow water where, should it sink, your rescue and the boat's salvage will be relatively easy.

TIP Some leaks are more annoying than threatening — someone left a hatch open, for example, and it's letting in spray. Still, water (and especially salt water) is not good for many boat systems, such as the electronics. Keep hatches and ports firmly closed when under way.

One of the first places to look if a boat has a leak is in the bilge where the propeller shaft exits the hull.

STEERING FAILURE

When wheel steering fails, you'll have a couple of moments of being puzzled before you realize that the boat is not responding when you turn the wheel. First, ensure that the autopilot has not been accidentally engaged, then locate and attach the emergency tiller. If you are able to steer again (it won't be easy), you know you still have a rudder and the problem is with the steering system.

Because of limited space in the cockpit, the emergency tiller is often too short to be easily handled. A common technique to get more leverage is to run lines from the tiller to the primary winches on the cockpit coamings.

REMEDIES

A wheel-steering system has several potential failure points. A cable connection may have come undone, a cable may have parted, or a cable may have stretched and fallen off the quadrant. In a rare case, the quadrant itself may have come loose on the rudder stock.

If it's a problem with the cable, it's repairable if the right tools and parts are on board.

If you can't effect a repair on the spot, steer the boat with the emergency tiller. Rigging lines from it to the primary winches will give you more purchase, and you might find it easier to steer when motoring than when sailing.

If the problem is with the rudder (or the rudder is missing), you can try steering with the sails, but that's easier said than done. Fortunately, rudders are generally pretty robust and solidly installed so, unless you hit something with it, you are unlikely to lose it.

If the boat should lose its rudder, adjust the sails (or furl them) to make the boat as comfortable as possible and call for help. Be prepared to set the anchor if the situation permits or requires that you do so.

FOULED PROPELLER

Floating debris, fishing traps of various kinds, and even seaweed lie in wait for boat propellers. Sailors sometimes inadvertently contribute their own lines to a boat-stopping wrap-up.

SYMPTOMS

You'll know your propeller is fouled if:

- The engine suddenly stops.
- The boat slows noticeably.
- You hear a slapping noise coming from under the boat.
- A line trailing over the side suddenly becomes taut.

RESPONSE

If the engine is still running, slow it down immediately, take it out of gear, and stop it. Look around the deck to see if a line has slipped over and become wrapped around the prop. Try to look under the boat to see the problem.

If the line around the prop leads back on board, put the gearshift in neutral so the prop is free to turn and try pulling on the line by hand. Don't use a winch.

If you can get to it, try turning the prop shaft manually from inside the boat while someone pulls on the line.

If you are caught by some kind of fishing trap line and can't free it, you'll have to haul up the line with a boathook, cut it, then try to clear the prop.

Kelp around the prop might clear on its own or with a little help from someone using a boathook from the deck, the dinghy, or the swim ladder.

If you are unable to clear the prop from on board, assess your options. If you have wind, sail toward home and call ahead to the marina or club for help getting the boat into its berth when you get there. If you have no wind, call for a tow, but use the sails to maintain control of the boat to the best of your ability.

....

TIP *If your motor is an outboard, tilt it up and clear the prop. Be careful — reaching that far behind the boat can be tricky. Make sure you are tethered to the boat.*

....

RIGGING FAILURE

Rigging failures take many forms. They can slow you down or end your sailing for the day. Shrouds and stays are under constant stress and subject to vibration while sheets and halyards suffer all manner of wear and tear. And then there's those darn shackles and pins holding it all together (or not, when Murphy has his way).

HALYARDS

If a halyard breaks or its shackle releases, the sail's luff will go slack. You'll have to pull down the sail and rehoist it on a spare halyard, if you have one available.

If you don't have a spare halyard, stow the sail and continue under the sail you have remaining. If the shackle simply let go, a rigger or boatyard worker will have to go aloft to retrieve the halyard after you get back to the dock.

SHEETS

If a jibsheet parts, it will most likely do so when you are on the wind and it is heavily loaded. Tack the boat so you can control the sail with the other sheet. You can then tie in a new sheet (if you can safely reach the clew) or furl the sail and replace the sheet when you get home.

If the mainsheet lets go, head up into the wind so the boom comes over the cockpit. Carefully, as the boom will be bouncing around, tie a strong line to the end of the boom. Haul the line taut and make it fast (maybe to a deck cleat) so you can control the boom while you drop and stow the sail.

STANDING RIGGING

Should you ever have a failure in the standing rigging, your most important concern is keeping the rig up. Once you've done all you can toward that end, head for home or somewhere closer where a permanent repair can be made.

If a shroud or a stay lets go you'll hear a loud bang, the mast will move and will no longer be straight. If the mast doesn't immediately fall down, you must act fast.

■ Shroud fails: If the shroud that failed was on the windward side, tack the boat to put the load on the opposite side. Attach a spare halyard to a strong point on the deck near the broken shroud and tension it with a winch. Drop the sails and motor home.

■ Backstay fails: Turn upwind and sheet the mainsail in hard so its leech supports the mast. Drop or furl the jib. Before you drop the mainsail, run a spare halyard to a strong point at the stern and winch it taut.

■ Forestay fails: Turn downwind and ease the mainsheet. The luff of the jib will support the mast temporarily while you rig a spare halyard to the stemhead to stand in for the stay. Put as much tension as you can on this halyard.

If the jib is on hanks, drop it as soon as you have a temporary stay rigged. If it's on a furler, try furling it. The halyard and sail will help support the mast. If you have difficulty furling it with a slack forestay, drop it — again after you've rigged the backup forestay. This will be tricky because you'll have to capture the broken stay as you gather the sail on the foredeck. Once it's down, use the halyard as a backup to the backup.

DISMASTING

Offshore sailors need a plan in case of a dismasting. Sailors at the ASA103 level would normally be within reach of assistance, so here's the drill:

■ Do **not** start the engine — there will be a mess of lines in the water, one of which will surely foul the propeller.

■ Call for assistance, and make a Securité call on VHF 16 to advise other vessels of your location and inability to maneuver.

■ Make sure everyone is wearing a PFD.

■ Keep everybody safe and prevent damage to the hull.

■ Try to maneuver the boat so the rig is to windward, so it acts as a sea anchor and not as a battering ram.

Donna Lange encountered many mishaps in the course of her singlehanded circumnavigation, but resourcefulness and singlemindedness saw her through to a successful return to Rhode Island in May, 2007.

FIRE

Fire aboard is possibly the sailor's greatest fear. Should it become established, it can destroy the boat. It can also inflict serious injury. Because there is no escaping it, you have to fight it. If it takes hold, you might have to abandon the boat.

FIRST RESPONSE

To assure the immediate safety of the crew, assemble everyone in an area as far upwind of the fire as possible and make sure they are wearing life jackets.

- Grab all the fire extinguishers.
- Grab the bucket with its lanyard.
- Retrieve the emergency flares from their locker.
- Retrieve the handheld VHF radio (if you have one) and switch it on.
- Grab any cell phones you can.
- Start fighting the fire.

TIP To improve your chances of successfully extinguishing a fire, carry more than the regulation number of extinguishers. Install them strategically so a fire in any location won't deny you access to all of them.

FIGHTING THE FIRE

Fight the fire from a position from which you can escape. Don't let the fire get between you and your exit.

Discharge the fire extinguisher in short bursts, aiming at the base of the flame and sweeping from side to side. Try to conserve the extinguishing material in the extinguisher but use enough to get the job done.

A fast-response vessel like this one is equipped to render assistance in many types of emergency.

Back up the extinguishers with the bucket. Use water on wood, fabric, and fiberglass but not on burning liquids.

TIP Know how to use the fire extinguishers. Read and memorize the instructions on the labels . . . and check their readiness gauges on a regular basis.

CALL FOR HELP

Fire is dire. Make an emergency call on VHF 16: Mayday if you have to abandon ship; Pan Pan if the boat is just disabled.

You can always call to stand down responders if you extinguish the fire and can get the boat and crew to safety.

Set off flares to attract the attention of boats within sight.

CAUSES OF FIRE ABOARD

By a wide margin, the major cause of fire aboard boats is electricity. Faulty wiring or electrical devices can overheat and ignite nearby combustible materials.

Engine-compartment fires are next on the list, caused by fuel leaks near hot components and electrical devices.

Cooking is low on the list. Many galley fires result from the use of alcohol fuel — because the flame from burning alcohol is hard to see, people sometimes don't realize it's burning. An alcohol fire is extinguishable with water, but burning alcohol will float on water — if it gets into the bilge, the fire might spread unseen.

TIP A smoke detector can be a lifesaver on a boat just as in a building.

FIRE ACCELERATORS

Cruising sailboats often have aboard combustible liquids, such as acetone, kerosene, and alcohol. Reduce the hazard they present by storing them in a locker isolated from ignition sources.

Few sailboats have gasoline inboard engines anymore but many smaller ones have outboards and larger ones carry gas for dinghy outboards.

Gasoline vapor forms an explosive mixture with air at room temperature and, because it's heavier than air, settles at low points in the hull. A tiny spark will ignite it. Gasoline must be stored with care and in such a way that fumes cannot get into the interior of the boat.

LPG (aka propane) cooking fuel can form an explosive mixture with air and is heavier than air. It must be stored in a locker that vents and drains to the exterior of the hull. Propane is given a distinctive odor so you can easily detect it.

Diesel fuel does not form an explosive mixture with air at normal temperatures but it will burn furiously once ignited. Fire risk aside, diesel's evil odor is a powerful incentive to clean up spills that occur during maintenance.

TIP If you smell gasoline or propane on boarding the boat, do not operate any electric switch or strike a match. Open the hatches and get off the boat. After 15 minutes, re-board and turn on the bilge blower. If you still smell fumes, look for the source or call a mechanic to trace it.

MAN OVERBOARD

In ASA101, you learned the Figure Eight and the Broad Reach-Close Reach methods for sailing the sailboat back to a crew who has fallen overboard. In the pages that follow, you'll find a few more techniques that take advantage of your more advanced skills.

BE PREPARED

Maneuvering the boat is only part of the MOB recovery operation. It's just as important to make proper use of available equipment to help locate the MOB and keep him afloat.

PFD

WHISTLE   PERSONAL STROBE

TYPE IV PFD

A PFD is a lifesaver. With a whistle and a light, a MOB can be heard and seen. A Type IV PFD used as a cockpit cushion is ready at hand if needed.

THROWABLE EQUIPMENT

Federal regulations require every sailboat over 16 feet long to carry a USCG-approved Type IV throwable PFD. Among the products that fill this requirement are a square cushion with arm bands, a life ring, or a horseshoe buoy. Most boats carry more than one device.

A horseshoe buoy or life ring is usually carried in a bracket on the stern pulpit from which it can be quickly released. A cushion is even easier to deploy, especially if you are sitting on it in the cockpit.

These devices can provide flotation to the MOB but do not add significantly to his visibility from the boat, especially in big seas. For this reason, sailboat racing rules require boats taking part in offshore races to carry a MOB pole. This consists of a long (as tall as 14 feet) fiberglass pole with a flag at the top and a float and weight at the base to keep it upright. If a race involves sailing at night, automatic lights that can be thrown to the MOB are also required.

This equipment is equally useful when cruising, and several variations on the MOB pole are available, including self-inflating devices that combine flotation for the MOB with a high-visibility inflating pole.

PERSONAL EQUIPMENT

The best piece of personal gear to be wearing should you be unfortunate enough to fall overboard would be your PFD. Whether it has fixed flotation, is auto-inflating, or is manual-inflating is a personal choice, but you should make sure you have, at the very least, a whistle attached to it and a strobe light to attract attention in poor visibility.

RECOVERY EQUIPMENT

Once you have brought the boat back to the MOB, your next task is to attach him to the boat.

Part of your recovery preparation is to make up a line with a bowline in one end (see next page). Throwing this line accurately will likely be a challenge and it could sink before the MOB can reach it. You might do better with a length, say 75 to 100 feet, of light floating line with a weight tied to one end. Floating line will be easier for the MOB to get hold of and you can pass him the bowline once you've hauled him close to the boat. (Marine catalogs and stores sell a variety of devices designed to serve this purpose.)

Many boating organizations hold the LifeSling® (see page 147) in high regard.

This boat is carrying a man-overboard pole on the backstay, a horseshoe buoy, and a LifeSling.

ONE GOAL: RECOVER THE MOB

When you have a person in the water, your only goal is to recover him or her as quickly as you can safely do so. Achieving that involves the same steps no matter the circumstances.

FIRST RESPONSE: "Y, T, P, S, C"
- **Yell** to alert the crew.
- **Throw** a Type IV or any other bouyant device toward the MOB.
- **Point** to keep the MOB in sight.
- **Set** the MOB button on the GPS.
- **Call** on VHF 16.

After that, everyone's attention (apart from the spotter, whose job it is to keep the MOB in sight) turns to the goal of getting the boat to the MOB, attaching the MOB to the boat, and bringing the MOB back aboard.

STEPS TO RECOVERY
Whoever sees the MOB go overboard must yell, "Man overboard!" or "Crew overboard!" or "Bobby overboard!" and repeat it until everyone aboard is aware of the situation.

At the same time, he must not let the MOB out of sight while he and others throw life rings, horseshoe buoys, even cockpit cushions toward the MOB. The more stuff in the water the better, to provide flotation to the MOB and to create a field of objects to aid in keeping his whereabouts in sight.

At the earliest opportunity, someone should set the MOB button on the GPS. This will record the boat's position the instant the button is pressed, giving you a location to sail back to if you lose sight of the MOB. You can also provide this position to responders when you call your emergency over VHF 16.

While the spotter points to the MOB — with a fully extended arm so everyone can see where he's pointing — the skipper must decide on the maneuver that will best bring the boat back to the MOB on **a close-reaching course**. The skipper must also assign tasks to the crew.

TIP *Watching and pointing to the MOB is crucial because as soon as the boat turns to begin the recovery maneuver, the crew, busy at their stations, will lose their orientation with respect to objects outside the boat.*

BROADCASTING ON CHANNEL 16

Any man-overboard situation is potentially life threatening. While your first priority is to bring the boat to the MOB and attach a line to him, call for help on VHF Channel 16 at the earliest possible opportunity.

If you have the situation under control, you can broadcast a "Pan-Pan, all stations" call to alert vessels in the area to the fact you are maneuvering to recover a man overboard. You can also call the Coast Guard directly. Either call will get the attention of other vessels and might well elicit an offer for help, say from someone nearby in a fast, low-freeboard powerboat who could render valuable assistance in recovering the MOB from the water.

If you have reason to believe the MOB is injured, or you lose sight of him, or the water is cold, call "Mayday."

Once you have the MOB safely aboard and have determined that no medical intervention is necessary, you can make another "All stations" call to advise the Good Samaritans on the water, thank you, but you no longer need their assistance. They will be pleased to hear the good news.

One of those tasks is to prepare a recovery system for getting the MOB back aboard. Essential to this is a long line with a bowline big enough to pass around the victim's torso tied in one end. You will use this to attach the MOB to the boat prior to recovering him from the water.

As the boat sails back to the MOB, someone can make the emergency call on VHF 16 (see box) giving the boat's position and the nature of your distress: person in the water. Most rescue boats, including those of commercial assistance services, have trained crews and special medical equipment and are capable of high speeds.

TIP *If you announce your position with reference to an ATON or geographic feature ("Two miles east of Tupelo Point," e.g.), that will mean more to nearby boats than a latitude and longitude from the GPS.*

A well rehearsed crew will instantly respond to the call, "Man overboard" with the Yell, Throw, Point, Set, Call routine.

QUICK STOP

The advantage of the Quick Stop over the Figure Eight and Broad Reach-Close Reach methods you learned in ASA101 is that the boat stays closer to the MOB. **But it has a downside: It involves jibing. For this reason, it should only be used by a well-practiced crew and in light to moderate winds. The crew must be able to quickly jump to the mainsail and safely execute the jibe while avoiding the added risk of an uncontrolled jibe.**

In this maneuver, from an upwind course, you turn the boat head to wind, tack, then steer in a circle back to the MOB.

① **Y, T, P, S, C.**

② Turn the boat head to wind and tack. Leave the jibsheet cleated so the backed jib pushes the boat through the tack.

③ Bear away to a broad reach with the jib backed and , if the boat will do it (this is what practice is for!), with the mainsail trimmed to centerline.

④ When the MOB is just abaft the beam, haul in on the mainsheet and jibe.

⑤ Cast off the jibsheet so the sail luffs.

⑥ If you have hands available, furl the jib. If not, it can wait until you have the MOB attached to the boat.

⑦ Continue to turn the boat to bring it on a close reach toward the MOB. Trim the mainsail or let it luff to control your speed.

⑧ Luff the mainsail to stop the boat just to windward of the MOB.

⑨ Attach the MOB to the boat and prepare for the recovery stage.

TIP In moderate winds, even with the jib backed, the boat might resist turning downwind in Step 3 with the mainsail sheeted to centerline. If that proves to be the case, ease the mainsheet to reduce the weather helm and increase boat speed to give the rudder more bite. Be ready to trim it back in for the jibe.

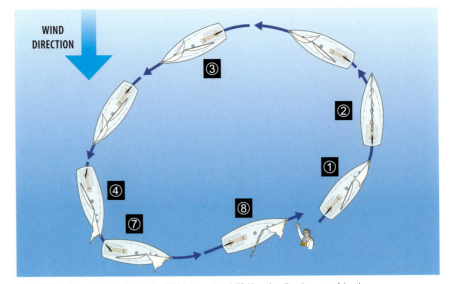

The Quick Stop keeps the boat close to the MOB but requires skillful boat handling because of the jibe.

PRACTICE BOAT HANDLING

As well as improving the chances of a happy outcome if someone falls off your boat, practicing MOB return and recovery techniques will also make you and your crew better sailors.

Successful execution of a MOB maneuver requires skillful boat handling. That means knowing how the boat will respond to actions you take with the helm and with the sails.

Design differences in hulls, keels, rudders, and sails affect how boats perform in close-quarters maneuvers. Whenever you skipper a boat that's new to you, one of the first things to do, for your enjoyment and your safety, would be to learn as quickly as you can how it handles under sail and under power.

When sailing, tack the boat a few times to see how quickly it slows down, tacks, and accelerates, as that will influence how you conduct a MOB recovery maneuver. Put the boat in irons and practice getting under way again. Practice jibing. Try sailing under just the mainsail and under just the jib.

When motoring, check the direction of prop walk in astern. Also test how the boat responds to the steering at faster and slower speeds.

Try out all these maneuvers, then put them together in practice MOB drills.

Don't practice MOB recovery on a live crew. Too many things can go wrong. For a dummy, make a float that will be about as visible as a person in the water and is heavy enough it won't be blown by the wind. A pair of half-filled one-gallon water jugs tied together works well and you can retrieve your homemade "Dunkin" with a boathook.

WHAT ABOUT THE SAILS?

You need the sails to maneuver the boat back to where the MOB is in the water. Once you reach him, they might be more of a hindrance than a help, depending on the weather conditions and how the boat handles.

Volunteer "victims" taking part in organized man-overboard exercises report that flailing jibsheets can be a hazard when the boat is to windward. For this reason the jib should be furled before the boat makes contact with the MOB - if you have crew available to do it.

The mainsail might steady the boat in rough seas, but you'll have to drop it if the boat sails too fast. Some boats might lie hove-to quietly and require little attention while the crew recovers the MOB from the water.

Every situation and every boat is different. This is why it's crucial to practice these maneuvers and learn which ones best suit your boat and your crew.

MOB WHEN MOTORING

When you are motoring with no sails up, you don't have to deal with the sails so, while the helmsman and spotter work together to bring the boat back to the MOB, everyone else can prepare for the recovery stage.

HEAD TO WIND

Although you are motoring, the wind is still a factor. Once you stop the boat to begin the recovery, the wind will take over. The best approach is from downwind, as this lessens the risk of running over the MOB with the boat.

Another big concern is the propeller — keep it away from the MOB at all costs and don't let a line trail overboard and get wrapped around it.

① **Y, T, P, S, C**, and throttle the engine back to idle to slow the boat down.

....

TIP *Shifting into reverse to make an emergency stop might not be the best move. In the heat of the moment you might shift gears too quickly and, anyway, you need steerageway to maneuver the boat.*

....

② Clear the deck of jibsheet tails and other lines that could be kicked overboard, and of items that might get in the way.
③ Prepare the MOB attachment line and the recovery system.
④ Maneuver the boat to a position about three boat lengths downwind of the MOB.

....

TIP *Depending on how busy the crew is, this might be the first available opportunity to make the call on the VHF.*

....

⑤ Turn the boat and motor slowly upwind toward the MOB.
⑥ Stop the boat about a boat length short of the MOB, then nudge it toward him with short bursts in forward gear, as when approaching a mooring.
⑦ Let the boat coast to a stop so the MOB is just at the bow where a

crewmember can drop the attachment line to him with the instruction to pass the loop over his head and shoulders.

....

TIP *At the bow, the MOB is as far away as he can be from the propeller. It's better to stop short and inch forward than to approach too fast and risk overrunning the MOB.*

....

⑧ As soon as you have contact with the MOB, shift into neutral. As soon as he's attached, shut down the engine to eliminate the propeller hazard.

⑨ Bring the MOB aboard using whatever recovery technique works with your crew and the equipment available (see next page).
⑩ After recovery, and before putting the engine in gear and getting under way again, check around the boat to ensure no lines are hanging over the side to get caught in the propeller.

THE MOTORING OPTION

If need be, for lack of experience, lack of confidence, or lack of crew on board, you can always choose to use the engine for getting the boat to the MOB, even if you were sailing.

Your first action, after Y, T, P, S, C, would be to head up into the wind to slow the boat, then furl the jib and, depending on the conditions, the mainsail.

Before starting the engine, make sure no lines are trailing in the water.

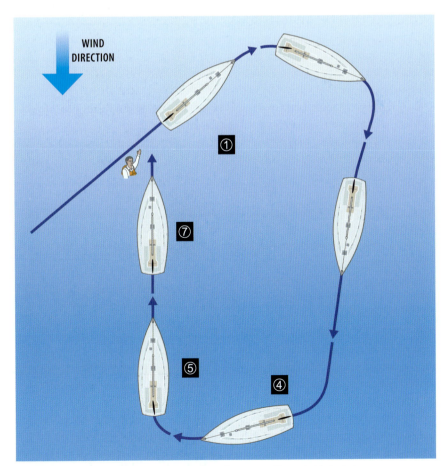

Turning the boat in the direction that will be helped by prop walk in astern could save valuable time in the recovery maneuver. This diagram shows the turn for a right-handed propeller, which helps turn the boat to starboard when in reverse gear.

BRINGING THE MOB BACK ON BOARD

Getting the boat back to the MOB is only one step in the recovery. Now you have to get him back aboard. That is not an easy proposition even when the MOB is alert, able to help himself, and fit. The boat's topsides present a high barrier and getting a grip on a wet person is difficult. If the water is cold, time is of the essence.

ASSESS THE MOB

Once you have the MOB alongside, you have to determine if he can help himself and to what degree. Most of the recovery methods described here assume that the MOB can respond to commands and perform some actions, even if he doesn't have the strength to get aboard unaided.

The first thing to do is get the MOB to pass his arms, head, and shoulders through the loop in the recovery line. He's now attached to the boat and you have a means of hauling him out of the water, albeit with considerable effort on his own part.

If the boat has no swim ladder, an agile MOB can get a lift aboard on the rope elevator.

SWIM LADDER OR SWIM STEP

If the boat has a swim ladder, and sea conditions permit, you might simply be able to deploy that and permit the MOB to climb back aboard with some dignity.

Many modern sailboats have a "walk-thru" transom that leads to a swim step from which a swim ladder can be lowered into the water. In calm sea conditions this step can provide a platform close to the water that a swimmer can grasp hold of and from which crew can reach him to assist him back aboard.

In even a moderate sea, the rise and fall of the transom might make this method too dangerous, so use it with caution.

ROPE ELEVATOR

When the MOB is able to assist in his own recovery but a ladder is not available, the rope elevator can lift him to the point where crew can reach him from the deck.

To make the elevator, tie one end of a stout line to a midships cleat or to the base of a shroud. Drop a deep bight over the side and bring the other end up through the stern fairlead and to the jibsheet winch. While a crew holds the

MOB with the attachment line, guiding him so he can stand on the bight of the line (it needs to be deep enough he can stand upright in it), grind away on the winch. As soon as the MOB is able to reach the rail, he can steady himself and help in the process.

Keep grinding until he can get a knee on the deck and you can help him over the lifelines.

If the boat has a lifeline gate, open it and haul the MOB through it. That eliminates the extra effort (and possible risk) of having to lift him over the lifelines.

TIP *You can practice with the rope elevator when you anchor for a swim stop.*

USE THE DINGHY

Many cruising sailboats tow a dinghy, and it might be easier to first get the MOB into the dinghy.

One person (wearing a PFD) will have to get into the dinghy to assist the MOB. Meanwhile, the crew on deck, using the retrieval line, can maneuver the MOB toward the dinghy.

Most hard dinghies are not stable enough to support someone climbing over the side. The best place to climb aboard from in the water is over the transom, and even this might be tricky if the MOB needs assistance — if the dinghy is small, the weight of two people in the stern might be too much. An outboard motor will present another obstacle.

Inflatables are stable enough you can haul a person in over the side. An inelegant but effective technique is to kneel against the tube, grasp the swimmer under the arms and around the chest, and push backward. With luck, you'll both end up in a laughing heap in the bottom of the dinghy.

If the water is warm and the swimmer unhurt, the most stressful part of the recovery is now over, but you still have to get aboard the sailboat from the dinghy. Don't release the MOB from the retrieval line until he's aboard the sailboat as the crew can use it to assist him.

TIP *All these recoveries are much easier if the MOB is wearing a life jacket.*

THE LIFESLING®

Many sailboats carry a LifeSling. Its principal feature is a flotation collar that's attached to the boat by a 125- to 150-foot length of floating line. The collar also serves as a sling for lifting the MOB out of the water. The LifeSling has been used successfully in many MOB recoveries and the ASA suggests its use as a valuable tool.

LIFESLING MANEUVER

The LifeSling does not replace the flotation you throw in response to the MOB alarm because it's tied to the boat and you will tow it away from the MOB. Instead, you deploy it as you make your return toward the MOB, then maneuver the boat around the MOB in an elliptical course to bring the floating line within his grasp. Using the LifeSling eliminates the need to stop the boat precisely at the MOB, which is diifficult to do at any time.

If your boat is equipped with a LifeSling, make sure your crew read the instructions printed on the case and, as important, understand the role of the MOB in the procedure. If the boat is in a shared-use arrangement, inspect the LifeSling each time you go sailing. Flake, don't coil, the floating line into the container to ensure it will deploy properly — and make sure it's secured to the boat.

If you were to perform the Quick Stop return, you would deploy the LifeSling as soon as your maneuver permitted.

The LifeSling recovery device is visible on many boats.

① **Y, T, P, S, C.**
② Turn the boat head to wind and tack but leave the jibsheet cleated so the jib is aback.
③ Deploy the LifeSling.
④ Bear away to a broad reach with the jib backed and the mainsail eased.
⑤ When the MOB is just abaft the beam, haul in on the mainsheet and jibe. Leave the jib sheeted in tight.
⑥ Sail the boat to leeward and within a boat length of the MOB. Control the boat's speed by trimming and easing the mainsheet but maintain enough speed that you can tack.
⑦ Tack and sail to windward of the MOB on a beam reach. Watch the path the LifeSling is making through the water.

TIP *You might be able to leave the jib aback for this step or you might have to let go the sheet — that's what practice is for!*

⑧ Jibe and sail close to leeward of the MOB. The goal is to drag the LifeSling so its line passes over the MOB.
⑨ If the MOB is able to grasp the line, luff up, stop the boat, and douse the sails. If not, make another circuit.
⑩ Haul the MOB toward the boat and prepare for the recovery stage.

TIP *If you don't have a LifeSling, you can MacGyver a towable device by tying a length of floating line to a float cushion or a horseshoe buoy.*

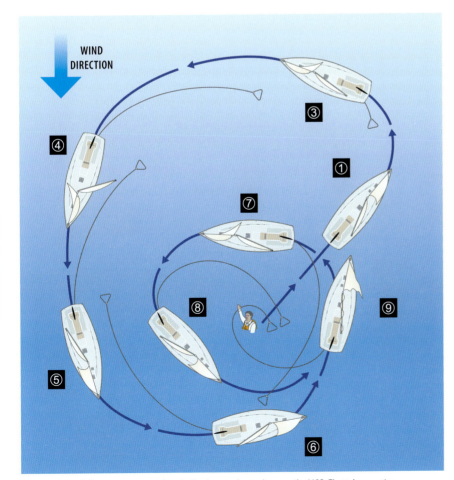

WIND DIRECTION

The goal of the LifeSling maneuver is to drag the floating attachment line over the MOB. That takes practice.

WHAT TO DO IF YOU FALL IN THE WATER

Thus far, the discussion about recovering a man overboard has been in the third person, but what if that person were you? As with any other emergency aboard, if you've thought about the possibility ahead of time, you will know what steps you can take to help in your own rescue.

Holding the limbs together in the H.E.L.P. position helps preserve the the body's heat.

MAKE NOISE

Yell like mad to make sure somebody notices that you fell and wave your arms to catch the attention of eyes on deck.

If you have taken the prudent approach to sailing, you will have a life jacket securely attached to your upper body. If it is of the type with an inflating mechanism and it didn't inflate automatically, activate it by hand or orally inflate it. Then grab the whistle that's attached to it and use it.

If you were not wearing your PFD, think about what you might jettison — boots, shoes, knife — anything to gain buoyancy.

WATCH THE BOAT

If the crew are following procedure, they will have thrown you a variety of flotation aids. If you can, swim toward these objects and gather them together to make the biggest possible target for the spotter to look for and latch onto.

You won't be encouraged to see the boat sailing away, but you know from practicing man-overboard recovery drills it's part of the maneuver that allows the boat to sail back toward you from the best direction. Meanwhile, ensure that the crew doesn't lose sight of you. Keep waving and blowing your whistle.

PROTECT YOURSELF

In cooler water, you must preserve your body heat. Even early-stage hypothermia will sap your strength and make it more difficult for you to help in your own rescue. Once you know the onboard spotter is locked on to you, try to move as little as possible and adopt the Heat Escape Lessening Position (H.E.L.P.). Hold your legs together and clasp your arms to your chest to minimize the area of your body in contact with cold water.

DONNING A LIFE JACKET IN THE WATER

If you weren't wearing a lifejacket, someone on the boat should throw you one as soon as the boat is close enough. You'll want to get into it so you can devote your energy to getting back aboard instead of just staying afloat.

Different designs of life jacket require different techniques for getting into them. You can practice these techniques in a swimming pool or simulate them on the dock. Your sailing instructor may offer additional hints.

Flip method for types I and III
Types I and III have flotation back and front and closures in the front.
1. Open the life jacket and turn it so the inside is facing upward.
2. Turn the life jacket so the shoulder portion is facing you. Grip both shoulders.
3. Flip the jacket over your head, release the shoulders, and slide your arms into the armholes. Your arms will be up at this point.
4. As you move your arms down, push the life jacket back down behind you and lean back onto it.
5. Once you're lying on the life jacket, floating face up, pull the sides around you to access the straps or zipper and fasten it. If the jacket has a crotch strap, secure it.

Keyhole entry for type II
Type II has flotation on the front and behind the head and a strap to hold it to the body.
1. Turn the life jacket so the head hole is toward you.
2. Put your head through the hole and pull the neck pad behind your head.
3. Float your body up so you're floating in the water on your back.
4. Pull the body strap around your back and ribs to tightly fasten the floats to your chest.

A life jacket doesn't just keep you afloat, it raises you a little out of the water, making you more visible, and you don't have to expend energy to keep your head above water.

HYPOTHERMIA AND TREATMENTS

Hypothermia occurs when the body cools excessively. Symptoms begin when the body's core temperature dips only a few degrees (to around 95° F), and that can happen after a relatively short immersion in water not much cooler than your core temperature. Even in the tropics, you can suffer from early-stage hypothermia if you get drenched and have no way of getting dry. Hypothermia develops in degrees, and victims are often unaware of their condition. It's important to be able to identify the symptoms in others.

STAGE 1 — MILD HYPOTHERMIA

Symptoms:
- violent shivering
- slurred speech

First-aid
- Remove wet clothing and wrap the patient in a blanket to cover the torso, thighs, head, and neck. A person at this stage should produce enough body heat to overcome the hypothermia. Watch for any change in the victim's condition.
- Give a patient who is awake and coherent warm (not hot) liquids.
- Do not give alcohol to a hypothermic person. Alcohol causes a release of body heat that will make the person feel warmer briefly but does not contribute to recovery.

STAGE 2 — MODERATE HYPOTHERMIA

Symptoms:
- loss of muscle control
- drowsiness
- incoherence
- exhaustion

First-aid
- The body cannot generate enough heat to warm itself. Removing wet clothing is essential but simply wrapping a person in blankets will not be enough to re-warm him. It will take an external source. Wrapping the patient in a blanket or a large sleeping bag together with a non-hypothermic person is the best method. Cover the patient's head.
- Do not massage the patient's arms

COLD SHOCK

A more immediate threat than hypothermia to a person who becomes immersed in cold water is cold shock. This can cause a sudden intake of breath, acceleration of the heart rate, and increase in blood pressure. If that involuntary gasp occurs under water, the victim is in danger of drowning — long before hypothermia becomes an issue. In vulnerable people, the heart activity can lead to cardiac problems.

The obvious lesson is: Stay on board. When sailing in waters colder than 60 degrees, wear insulating clothing. Dinghy sailors do this as a matter of course. It may not prevent cold shock but it will retard hypothermia.

and legs. Warm the trunk of the body first. The body keeps vital organs warm by holding warm blood in the core. It does this by constricting blood vessels in the extremities to prevent cold blood from flowing back and cooling the core. Rubbing them could cause cold blood to flow from the arms and legs to the heart, possibly causing heart arrhythmia.
- Do not administer fluids and certainly not alcohol.

STAGE 3 — SEVERE HYPOTHERMIA

Symptoms:
- Collapse
- Unconsciousness
- Heart failure
- Respiratory failure

First-aid
- Severe hypothermia is a medical emergency. Call the Coast Guard or any other appropriate or available source of assistance if a hypothermia patient is not responding to treatment.

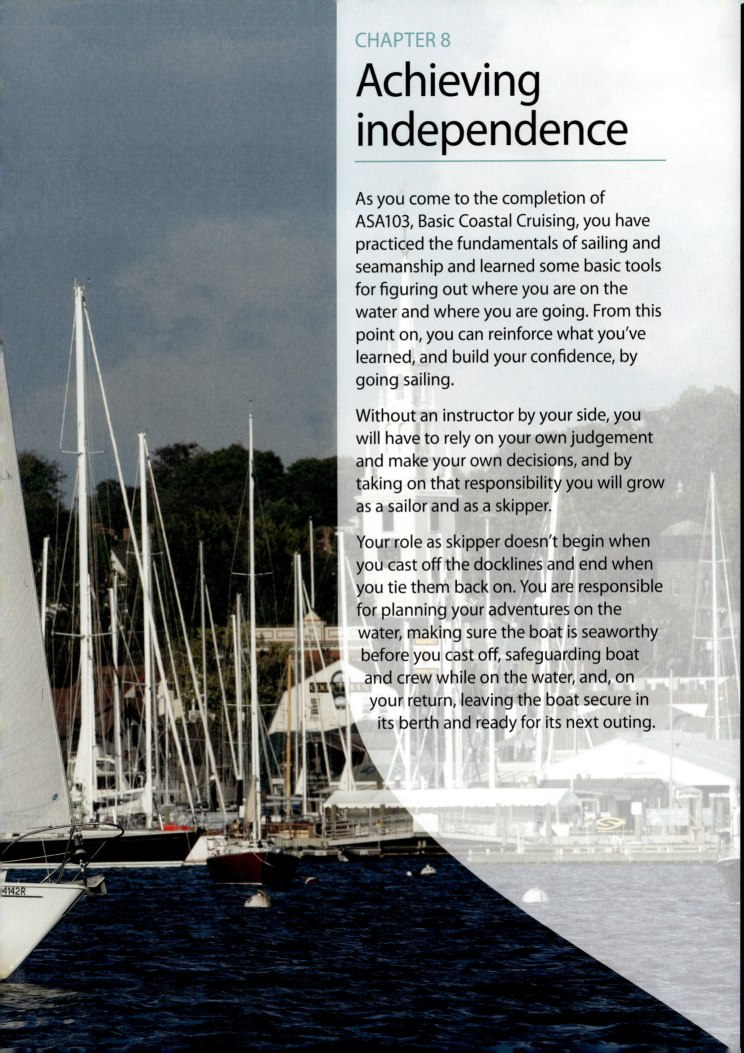

CHAPTER 8

Achieving independence

As you come to the completion of ASA103, Basic Coastal Cruising, you have practiced the fundamentals of sailing and seamanship and learned some basic tools for figuring out where you are on the water and where you are going. From this point on, you can reinforce what you've learned, and build your confidence, by going sailing.

Without an instructor by your side, you will have to rely on your own judgement and make your own decisions, and by taking on that responsibility you will grow as a sailor and as a skipper.

Your role as skipper doesn't begin when you cast off the docklines and end when you tie them back on. You are responsible for planning your adventures on the water, making sure the boat is seaworthy before you cast off, safeguarding boat and crew while on the water, and, on your return, leaving the boat secure in its berth and ready for its next outing.

PLANNING A SHORT CRUISE

Few moments can top the sensation of euphoria, anticipation, and apprehension that accompany untying the docklines and setting off on your first cruise. So the intoxication of the moment doesn't turn into a hangover, though, spend a little time and energy thinking about where you'll go, how you'll get there, and how you will know you are there when you arrive. A little planning will relieve the anxiety and amplify the fun.

WHERE

So, the boat will sail at 5 knots, we can get in eight hours of sailing from 8 a.m. to 4 p.m., so we'll plan on about a 40-mile round trip . . . maybe not.

First of all, this is a sailboat, and at times will sail at 5 knots indeed, but not necessarily in the direction you had planned to go. And you have to maneuver out of the marina to open water just to get to mile zero. Reckon on 20 miles for a long day. And eight hours is a long day on the water for anyone. All that sun and wind take their toll and fatigue is not a good shipmate.

Study the chart of your cruising ground and mark a sequence of potential destinations within a radius of 10 miles or less. It's not a sign of weakness or lack of commitment to plan easy days — if you get to your destination early, you can fill the extra time with sailing practice.

Read the cruising guides to the region to learn about possible anchorages or marinas where you can stop for lunch if you want to. Plot the locations of good candidates on the chart.

HOW

Draw the courses you expect to sail on the chart, write down their directions according to the compass rose (using the parallel rule), and imagine how different winds will affect them. (You can even draw an arrow for the forecast wind right on the chart.)

Measure the length of each course and write that down next to its direction. Using the speed/time/distance formula, calculate the time you expect each leg will take to sail (doubling the time for windward legs). Add the times and adjust your itinerary so your total meets a

reasonable goal for a daysail. Then draw up an alternative itinerary in case the wind didn't read the weather forecast.

....

TIP *Start your cruising adventures in familiar waters. As you gain knowledge of the sailing area, its weather, and the boat, and your confidence as a sailor grows, you can make more ambitious plans.*

....

WHEN

Busy lives don't allow a lot of leeway for planning getaways but, obviously, you want to choose a time of year when the chances for fair weather are high.

Well ahead of your planned dates, start watching the extended forecasts to get a sense of how the weather is trending. If it appears a wet, windy low-pressure system is in the offing, try to postpone — the days that follow it will usually be sunny.

If your cruising grounds are tidal, watch the times of high and low tide to anticipate how they will affect your plans. If low tide means the only time you can exit your river is at 2 a.m., reschedule. Even if tide heights are not a factor,

A guide book that supplements information provided by the charts is a great help when planning a daysail.

PAPER CHARTS

In this age of electronic everything, some people think that paper charts are redundant. Far from it, and they are more than just a safety backup in case the electronics fail. To look at the big picture of your upcoming cruise, nothing beats spreading out a chart that shows your cruising area with all the critical detail that disappears from the chart plotter's screen when you zoom out. Make sure you have aboard detailed charts for the areas where you will be sailing.

currents might be — a 2-knot current takes a big bite out of a 5-knot sailing speed, and wind against current in an ocean inlet can create dangerous waves.

In areas where afternoon thunderstorms are likely to pop up, it pays to plan your outing so the boat can be secured (to a dock, a mooring, or its own anchor) before they burst upon the scene.

WHO

Skippering a sailboat is a responsibility. When you take along crew, they depend on you to conduct the boat competently and safely — and to bring them home at a reasonable time.

You will be spending the day in close quarters, so you'll want to choose your company carefully. Don't invite too many along as tending the lines is difficult in a crowded cockpit.

A good source for crew is your ASA sailing school. Ask about students who are at a similar or more advanced level than you — they will speak the same sailing language as you. You are still learning the ropes, so take along at least one experienced mate who can help out if things get stressful.

WHAT

What boat you sail and what you have to bring along depends on whether it's your boat, a charter boat, or a club boat.

If it's your boat, you will have fitted it out with all the recommended and required safety equipment and navigation tools, plus whatever gear you find useful or necessary.

A charter boat should have most of that equipment on board (and an inventory you can check ahead of time), but you might want to bring along some of your own sailing gear and equipment so you'll know you have it.

A club boat should also be equipped for normal use. After your first outing on it, you'll know what to bring, or leave at home, next time.

PROVISIONS

Sailing is hungry work and since our boat has lockers for storing food there's no reason not to keep a supply of non-perishables aboard. High-energy snack food like peanut butter, crackers, cookies, dried fruit, and your favorite energy bars are always good to have around in case the day on the water becomes extended by weather or other unplanned events.

It's important to stay hydrated when you're exposed to wind and sun, so bring a supply of drinking water (the water in the boat's tanks might not taste good). Bring other beverages, too, such as sodas and juice, to suit the preferences of your crew. Cans are preferable to bottles — boats rock and broken glass is not fun.

For meals, bring food that's easy to prepare, eat, and clean up after. If you bring it in a portable cooler you can carry the trash out in the same container at the end of the day.

You might want to bring along a roll of paper towels — and don't forget the toilet paper and trash bags.

....
TIP *Planning is a key part of the voyage. It's fun and a good way to involve your crew.*
....

Fair weather, a fun crew, a capable boat, and a plan are the ingredients for an enjoyable outing on the water.

PERSONAL SAILING GEAR

Cover photos of sailing magazines would have us believe that all anyone ever wears on a boat is shorts and a tee shirt, or a bikini. That's possibly true in the tropics, but in areas where the water stays cold, no matter what the air temperature is ashore, wind over water will generate a chill. If you get wet, you will feel colder even on a warm day.

CLOTHING AND EFFECTS

Prepare for all eventualites by bringing clothes that work in layers — sailing upwind and downwind in the same breeze on the same day you might think you were in different climates.

For clothing, think layers:

- Microfiber or cotton T-shirt and shorts
- Fleece pullover warm-up layer
- Water- and windproof jacket and pants to fend off spray and rain
- Wide-brimmed hat for sun protection.

You'll also want to bring:

- Boat shoes for traction on deck
- Sailing gloves
- Sunscreen
- A sailor's knife
- Your personal PFD

You won't need your valuables — wallet, purse, jewelry, phone — while you are sailing, so stow them in your bag. Don't leave anything lying around loose or it'll end up falling to the lowest spot it can find (where it might get wet).

TIP *Foul weather gear of excellent design and quality is available at reasonable prices at marine stores. Don't go mad — a deep-ocean suit is overkill for temperate-zone coastal cruising.*

TIP *Draw up a list of clothing and other items, perhaps broken down into "essential" and "nice-to-have-if-there's-room," and keep it in your seabag. You can add to the list (or scratch stuff off) as experience teaches you.*

YOUR PERSONAL SEABAG

Space aboard a sailboat it limited, so pack only what you need. A soft bag is best as it can be stuffed into the typically odd-shaped spaces found on a boat. A waterproof bag or one with a waterproof bottom will have obvious advantages if the boat has a tendency to be wet.

GUIDELINES FOR GUESTS

Any guests (a sailors' euphemism for slave crew) will need the same things you do, so if you have a list of what you like to bring aboard, share it with them.

If you will be the skipper, it's up to you to ensure the boat has the required safety equipment. Guests shouldn't need to bring any of that except perhaps a personal life jacket for the sake of comfort. Other valuable things guests can bring are great tunes, patience, and a sense of humor.

In the days before the cruise, share your planned itinerary with your guests and prepare them for what to expect from a day of fun aboard a sailboat.

TIP *Guests who have not sailed before will benefit enormously from watching the ASA's "Your First Sail" video (available at www.asa.com) for a preview of what to expect.*

TIP *If any of your crew takes regular medication, even if it's aspirin, advise them to bring supplies for the trip plus a day, just in case. And anyone with a medical condition should advise you about it and possible implications well ahead of time. Anyone taking seasickness medication should start several hours before boarding.*

Sometimes, a fine sailing breeze is accompanied by rain, and perhaps a bit of spray, so dress appropriately to stay dry and warm. And take extra dry clothes in case you get doused by a playful wave.

SKIPPER'S BRIEFING

When your guests or crew arrive aboard, take them on a tour of the boat, as in Chapter 1, describing the general layout and how everything works together. Give them an overview of the boat's systems and demonstrate operating the head and how to open and close hatches and portlights.

CREW ORIENTATION

Before you get under way, ensure everyone aboard is familiar with the locations and use of the boat's safety equipment. If you do this in a more formal manner, everyone will get that this is serious stuff. With luck, this will be the only time you'll have to act a little bit "skipperish."

■ Show the crew where the life jackets are stowed, offer one to each of them and, if necessary, demonstrate how to put one on.

■ Point out the fire extinguishers and read the operating instructions from the labels.

■ Do the same with the flares.

■ Turn on the VHF radio and demonstrate its basic operation — a well-run boat will have the protocol for making a call posted nearby.

■ Go over the itinerary for the day on the paper chart, giving courses, distances, approximate times, and noting any landmarks along the way.

■ On deck, point out the halyards, furling lines, sheets, vang, and any other sail controls, with instructions where necessary on how they function — even experienced crew might welcome enlightenment because every boat is rigged differently.

■ Finally, describe how you will be getting off the dock or out of the slip and assign tasks as needed.

TIP Point out to new crew the "danger areas" to avoid or where to exercise caution — the arc where the boom swings, the leeward sidedeck, the bow, the aft deck, and slick surfaces like the tops of hatches.

SAILING TO A NEW HARBOR

When you head out of your home port on a day sail for the first time, you have the great benefit of seeing all its salient features along the way. If you take the simple precaution of looking behind you from time to time on your way out, you will find you've taken a lot of stress out of the return trip.

Visiting a new harbor is something else. Unless your cruising guide has photographs, you may not have a clue about what it even looks like. This is where observation and a careful study of the chart pay off.

Before setting off, study your route on the chart and note the aids to navigation and landmarks along the way and the approximate times at which you will pass them (based on an estimate of the speed at which you will be sailing).

Look for features — breakwater, smokestack, high cliff — that will guide you to the harbor's entrance as you approach it. You might be able to use them as ranges to lead you to a point at which you can spot the channel markers, which can be hard to pick out against the background.

If you plan to stop at your destination, you'll have to figure out a good spot to take down the sails. You might be able to sail all the way in to a sheltered area or you might prefer to drop the sails outside and motor in . . . make whatever you think is the prudent choice. If you've done your planning, you will already know where you will be mooring or anchoring.

If the route into the harbor is along a winding channel, pay close attention to the sequence of channel markers. Check for current — make sure it's not setting you out of the channel. In unfamiliar waters, slow is better than fast.

On your way in to your new harbor, look behind from time to time. When you leave, you will be grateful for having had a preview of your exit route.

Before sailing to a new harbor, get the lay of the land (and the water), from charts, guidebooks, and Google Earth.

PUTTING THE SAILBOAT TO BED

When your day of sailing comes to an end and it's time to leave the boat in its berth for a day, or a week, or even longer, you want to know that it will stay where you tied it and not suffer damage in the event of bad weather. A few simple procedures and a checklist will help you ensure it stays shipshape and, what's more, is ready to go the next time you (or anyone else) want to take it for a sail.

SECURING TO A DOCK

When you came in from sailing, you might have done a quick job with the docklines and fenders before turning to other tasks like flaking and covering the mainsail. While the boat might be perfectly secure in the present weather conditions, a change in the wind's direction or strength could change that. Now's the time to square away the fenders and docklines.

SIDE TIE

If the boat will be lying alongside a floating dock, adjust the bow line, stern line, and spring lines to hold the boat parallel to it.

The bow line holds the bow in toward the dock and also holds the boat against moving back.

The stern line holds the stern in toward the dock and also holds the boat against moving forward.

If it were secured with only the bow and stern lines, the boat would still be free to rotate to some degree, which could cause a part of the hull unprotected by fenders to contact the dock.

Adding a forward spring line and an aft spring line limits the boat's ability to rotate. When the lines are equally

tensioned, the boat will move about significantly less than when they are not.

Where you tie the spring lines on the boat will depend on the hardware available on the boat and on the dock, but you want to ensure they don't foul the fenders and lift them out from between the hull and the dock.

Make sure you have enough fenders of an appropriate size strategically spaced along the middle third of the boat to handle situations when it isn't lying exactly parallel to the dock. There will be times, when the wind blows onto the dock, when the fenders will be working extra hard.

When a boat is lying alongside a quay or a pier where there is significant tidal range, the docklines need to be longer to accommodate the boat rising and falling with the tide.

CHAFING GEAR

One of the sailor's greatest enemies is *chafe*. Whenever a line or a sail rubs against a part of the rig or a part of the boat, it will suffer wear, or chafe. Docklines chafe where they pass through chocks or fairleads, especially if the dock is exposed to wind and waves, but you can protect them with chafing gear. What

Chafing gear protects docklines from wear caused by the boat moving under the influence of wind and waves.

you use depends on the seriousness of the problem and what you have available.

As a temporary fix for a rough night in an exposed dock, rags tied to a dockline at the point of chafe will suffice.

Sailors who keep their boats in the same slip all the time might affix chafing gear semi-permanently to docklines that stay at the slip when the boat is sailing. This gear may be plastic hose or even fire hose.

Whatever material is used, it has to allow the line to stretch and contract inside it. Nylon stretches considerably under load. This allows it to absorb shock loads, which makes it the favored material for docklines.

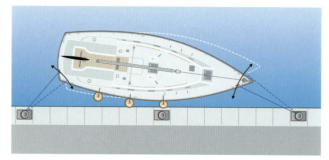

When tied with only a bow line and a stern line, a boat might not lie on its fenders if the effect of wind and/or current causes it to rotate..

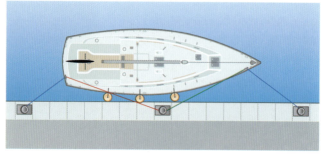

Properly secured with spring lines, the boat will lie squarely against its fenders , although it might shift a little forward or aft under the influence of wind and current.

TYING IN A SLIP

Slips come in many configurations. A basic slip has a piling at each corner and a short access pier off the main pier. A more elaborate slip might have a pier or float the length of one side.

To secure a boat in a basic slip, you need two bow lines (one each side), four spring lines (two each side), and two stern lines (one each side). When leaving the boat, you brace it with this network of lines so it's centered in the slip and can't blow forward, back, or to either side.

> **TIP** *If you set up the stern lines so you can lengthen or shorten them from the dock, you can adjust them so you can get on and off the boat, then square the boat in the slip when you leave.*

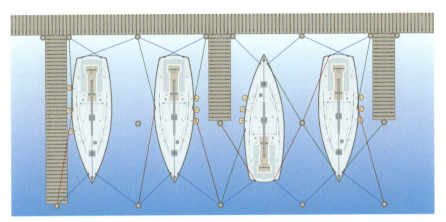

Securing a boat in a slip is an art, and how it's done depends on the prevailing weather as well as the slip's layout.

LINES ABOARD OR ASHORE

If you are staying aboard the boat, it makes sense that you would want to be able to adjust your docklines from on board, especially if the reason for doing so was that wind and waves were causing the boat to move in such a way that getting onto the dock would be difficult. In that case, you might place loops over cleats or pilings on the dock and bring the ends aboard.

If you will be leaving the boat and marina staff or others might need to tend your docklines for any reason, you want enough of each line ashore that they can adjust them without having to climb aboard. In this case, make tidy coils of your lines on the dock so people don't trip over them or accidentally kick them into the water.

Simple slips like these are common in regions where the tidal range is small. Boats must be secured so they don't contact each other, the piers, or the pilings.

SECURE THE BOAT: ON DECK

Before leaving the boat, you want to be assured that, when you return for your next and highly anticipated day of sailing, the boat and its equipment will be in good shape and ready for a prompt departure. As you put the boat to bed, inspect the sails and gear and arrange for defects to be attended to so they don't impinge on your sailing time or that of others who use the boat.

SAILS STOWED

- Flake or furl the mainsail on the boom (according to the practice on the boat) and put the mainsail cover on it.
- If the jib is hanked on to the forestay, unhank it, flake it, bag it, and stow it in its customary location.
- A strong wind can tear a loosely furled jib to shreds. Make sure any roller-furling jib is furled tightly and that no fabric is showing that is not protected by the UV cover strips on the leech and foot. If it's furled loosely, and wind conditions permit, unfurl it and refurl it. Don't leave the clew exposed — pull on the furling line until you have at least three wraps of the sheets around the sail. Secure the furling line and haul the jibsheets taut and secure them.

LINES SQUARED AWAY

- Detach the main halyard from the mainsail and shackle it to its normal storage location (on many boats that's the end of the boom).
- Visually check all the halyards to ensure they are not tangled or chafing on the mast or standing rigging.

....

TIP *It's good practice to shackle spare halyards to stanchion bases or other convenient points on the deck so they don't slap the mast when the wind blows. This protects them and the mast from damage and makes for quieter nights for neighbors.*

....

TIP *If the boat has tail bags, flake the lines into them, bitter ends first.*

....

Check that all sail control lines are secure. Flake their tails into bins or bags or coil them and hang them.

Ideally, you would like to protect running rigging from sunlight and airborne dirt, but much of it is permanently rigged so the best you can do is stow the lines where they are least exposed.

- Coil all the lines: jibsheets, furling line, and the various mainsail controls next to the companionway. Wherever possible, hang the coils, especially those that are not under cover, so dirt and dampness don't collect around them.

LOOSE GEAR

- Scout around the deck to retrieve any bits of equipment you might have used such as snatch blocks or the boathook and stow them in their proper places.
- Gather up the winch handles and any other valuable loose items from the cockpit and stow them safely so they don't "walk" off the boat in your absence.

ENGINE

- Make sure the gearshift is in neutral. If the boat has a start key, retrieve it from the engine control panel and place it in its proper place.

....

TIP *All lines, whenever possible, are best left coiled and hung so they can dry out after a rain. You don't want to deal with soggy piles of wet rope next time you come aboard.*

....

A boat that lives on a mooring is in some ways less at risk of damage than one in a marina. It is free to lie to the wind and needs no fenders. It might be more exposed to waves, so everything on deck and below must be buttoned up tight.

SECURE THE BOAT: BELOWDECKS

Just as you want everything on deck to be ready when you join the boat for your next sail, you would also like to find the cabin shipshape, all the systems working properly, and no surprise leftovers from the last meal eaten aboard. Running through a checklist before you close the boat up will go a long way toward ensuring that happens.

"A place for everything and everything in its place" is a good rule for keeping a boat tidy and safe.

ENGINE COMPARTMENT

■ Open the engine compartment and look around and under the engine for signs of water (from the cooling system perhaps) and oil drips. Use your nose — are there any smells you can't readily account for, such as diesel fuel or hot rubber.
■ Close the seacock on the engine raw-water intake.

TIP *Hanging the engine key on or near this seacock ensures you'll remember to open it next time you want to start the engine.*

■ If you used the engine to get back to the dock, now might be a good time to check the oil level. If needed, make a note to bring oil next time you use the boat.

BILGE AND PLUMBING

■ Lift a couple of floorboards and check the bilge for water.
■ Check the strainer on the bilge pump and clear any obstructions.

■ Test the bilge pump by flicking its switch from "Auto" to "Manual" and back.
■ Close the seacocks on the galley sink drain, head sink drain, and head intake.
■ Check the levels in the water tanks (and fill them if necessary).

HOUSEKEEPING

■ Stow all loose items — even at the dock, waves and boat wakes can cause stuff to move around and fall to the sole.
■ Make sure drawers and locker doors are firmly closed.
■ Close the cabin and head doors so they can't swing about if waves rock the boat.

TIP *If the cabin doors have hooks or other devices to hold them open, use them. That will improve ventilation in the cabins.*

■ If the boat has an icebox and you will not be coming back in the next day or so, empty it of food and ice, wipe the inside clean, and leave the lid open.

■ Close and secure all hatches and portlights, but make sure the deck vents are open so the boat can breathe.

ELECTRICAL

■ Switch off all circuits on the electrical panel and turn the battery switch to "Off." (The automatic bilge pump is normally wired directly to the battery, so will still operate if needed.)
NOTE If the boat has shorepower, whether it is left connected or not and, if it is, which circuits are to be left activated, is the decision of the instructor or skipper of the boat.

RECORD DEFECTS

■ Make notes of any defects and shortages you discover and arrange for them to be remedied by whoever is responsible for the upkeep of the boat.

TIP *Record maintenance needed and performed in the ship's log so the next crew coming aboard can see what has been done and what, if anything, remains on the "to do" list.*

ON DECK AGAIN

■ Check all the hatches are closed and, using the hose from the dock, hose down the deck and hull to remove salt and dirt.
■ Check the docklines and fenders again.
■ Take the trash and recyclables ashore and dispose of them in the proper receptacles, if provided, or take them home for disposal.

When a sailboat is to be unattended for any length of time, nothing should be left lying around that might fall.